# Women in Jainism

# Women in Jainism

*A Case Study of Gujarat Inscriptions*

**Mrinal Joshi**

**RAWAT PUBLICATIONS**

Jaipur • New Delhi • Bangalore • Mumbai • Hyderabad • Guwahati

ISBN 81-316-0255-9


*Published by*
Prem Rawat for **Rawat Publications**
Satyam Apts., Sector 3, Jawahar Nagar, Jaipur 302 004 (India)
Phone: 0141 265 1748 / 7006 Fax: 0141 265 1748
E-mail: info@rawatbooks.com
Website: www.rawatbooks.com

*New Delhi Office*
4858/24, Ansari Road, Daryaganj, New Delhi 110 002
Phone: 011-23263290

*Also at Bangalore, Mumbai, Hyderabad and Guwahati*

Typeset by Rawat Computers, Jaipur
Printed at Chaman Enterprises, New Delhi

*to my parents*
late Mr. V.M. Paranjpay
Meena Paranjpay

# Contents

# Abbreviations

*APJLS* : Muni, Jayantavijayji, ed. & comp., *Shri Arbuda Prachina-Jaina-Lekha Sandoha* (Ujjain, Shri Vijaydharmasuri Jaina Grantha Mala, 1937).

*HIG-V* : Shastri, H.G., Comp., *Historical Inscriptions of Gujarat* Vol. V, (Bombay, The Forbes Gujarati Sabha, 1981).

*JDLS-I* : Shri Buddhisagarsuriji, *Jaina Dhatu Pratima Lekha Sangraha,* Vol. I (Mumbai, Shri Adhyatma Jnana Prasaraka Mandala, 1917).

*JDLS-II* : Shri Buddhisagarsuriji, *Jaina Dhatu Pratima Lekha Sangraha* Vol. II (Padra, Adhyatma Jnana Prasaraka Mandala, 1924).

*JPLS* : Daulatsingh Lodha, 'Aravinda' ed. & trans., Acharya Yatindrasurishwarji, comp., *Shri Jaina Pratima Lekha Sangraha* (Dhanmaniya, Shri Yatindra Sahitya Sadana, 1951).

*NIR* : *Nirgrantha,* Vol. III, 1997–2002.

*PJLS-II* : Muni, Jinavijaya, ed. & comp., *Prachina Jaina Lekha Sangraha,* Part II, (Bhavnagar, Jaina Atmananda Sabha, 1921).

*PLS-I* : Muni, Vidyavijayaji, ed., *Prachina Lekha Sangraha,* part I, (Bhavnagar, Shri Yashovijay Jaina Grantha Mala, 1929).

*RPLS* : Muni, Vishalavijaya, ed., *Shri Radhanpura Pratimalekha Sandoha* (Bhavnagar, Shri Yashovijaya Grantha Mala, 1960).

| | |
|---|---|
| *Shat* | : Acharya Kanchansagarsuri, auth. & comp., Muni Pramodasagar ed., *Shri Shatrunjaya Giriraja Darshana ane Shilpa Sthapatya Kalamam Shri Shatrunjaya.* (Kapadwanj, Agmoddhara Grantha Mala, 1982). |
| *TSPC* | : Hemachandracharya's *Trishashtishalakapurushacharita*, trans., Helen Johnson, Vol. I-IV (Baroda, Oriental Institute). |
| *EI* | : *Epigraphia Indica* |

## Technical Abbreviations*

| | |
|---|---|
| Ba | : Bai, honorific epithet or name ending of ladies in Western India. |
| Bhan | : Bhandari |
| Do | : Doshi |
| Gan | : Gandhi** |
| Man | : Mantri |
| Maham | : Mahanta, a chief clerk |
| Pa | : Pandita/Parikh, an examiner of coins, a family name |
| Sa | : Sahu or sadhu, designation of a member of a mercantile community |
| San | : Sanghapati |
| Sha | : Shah |
| Shre | : Shreshti, a banker |
| Sudi/Shudi/Shu etc. | : Shulka-paksha-dina, a day of the bright fortnight |
| Tha | : Thakkura, Thakura |
| Vadi | : Vadya-paksha-dina, a day of the dark fortnight |
| Vya | : Vyavahari, merchant |
| Shri | : An honorific |

*Compiled from—*Indian Epigraphical Glossary*, by D.C. Sircar JDLS-I, JPLS, PLS.

**Not given in the above sources, but this seems to be the most likely explanation.

# Glossary of Indian Words

| | |
|---|---|
| *acharya* | head of a mendicant group, spiritual leader |
| *ahimsa* | non-violence; to be free from cruelty; to be compassionate to all |
| *anuloma* | a type of inter-caste marriage in which husband belongs to a higher caste |
| *aparigraha* | non-avarice; freedom from greed |
| *asteya* | non stealing |
| *bharya* | wife |
| *brahmacharya* | celibacy |
| *brahman* | a person of the priestly class/caste |
| *chakravartin* | universal monarch, one of the five categories of Great Men in Jaina Puranas |
| *chaturvinshatipatta/chaturvinshati-tirthankarapatta/chovishi* | a slab with the images of all the twenty-four Jaina *tirthankaras* |
| *dandanayaka* | a general; a leader of forces; an army officer; a military commander |

---

This Glossary has been prepared with the help of *Indian Epigraphical Glossary* of D.C. Sircar, *The Penguin History of Early India* by Romila Thapar, *Gender and Salvation* of Padmanabh S. Jaini, *Jaina Iconography* of U.P. Shah, and other works.

| | |
|---|---|
| *devakulika* | a supplementary or small shrine; a cell |
| *dharmapatni* | a wife by law |
| *dharmashala* | a rest house |
| *Digambara* | literally, 'sky-clad', one of the two main Jaina sects |
| *diwan* | chief administrator or finance minister |
| *duhita* | daughter |
| *farman* | royal order, proclamation |
| *gaccha* | an ascetic group of Jainas |
| *ganadhara* | chief disciple of a Jina |
| *gotra* | a family or clan, a tribe or lineage |
| *gruha-jamata* | son-in-law, who stays with the wife's family |
| *guru* | a teacher; spiritual preceptor |
| *Ibadatkhana* | name of the house built by Mughal emperor Akbar to hold discussions among leaders and saints of various religions |
| *Indra-Indrani* | king and the queen of gods |
| *jamata* | son-in-law |
| *kevalajnana* | supreme enlightenment; infinite knowledge; omniscience |
| *kshatriya* | a person of warrior class/caste |
| *kula* | family |
| *mahatirtha* | prominent among places of pilgrimage |
| *moksha* | spiritual liberation, salvation; freedom from rebirth |
| *muni* | a monk |
| *Murtipujaka* | a sub sect of the Jainas, which worships the images |
| *nagarashetha* | the chief merchant of the city |
| *paduka* | foot impressions |
| *panchatirthi/panchatirthapatta* | an image of five *tirthankaras*, one of whom is more prominent |
| *patni* | wife |
| *pattavali* | succession list of spiritual heads among the Jainas |
| *pinda* | a ball of rice offered to the manes |
| *prashasti* | eulogy |

*prtiloma* — an unapproved form of inter-caste marriage in which the husband belongs to the caste lower than that of the wife in social hierarchy

*pativrata* — a devoted wife for whom husband is a deity

*putri* — daughter

*Rajput* — a name of a warrior clan

*sadhu* — a monk

*sadhvi* — a nun

*sahagamana/samagama/sati* — self immolation by the widow on the funeral pyre of her husband

*samavasarana* — refers to the sermon hall constructed by gods, where heavenly beings, human beings and animals assemble, take their apportioned seats, and attend to the first sermon delivered by a tirthankara after enlightenment

*samvat* — an year, mostly of Vikrama era, one of the two most widely used eras of ancient and medieval India (beginning 58-57 B.C.E.); the other being Shaka era (beginning 78 C.E.)

*sangha* — the fourfold Jaina community consisting of the order of monks, nuns, laymen and laywomen.

*sanghapati* — one who arranges and sponsors the pilgrimage and leads a Jaina *sangha*

*sarthavahi* — wife of a *sarthavaha,* a trader, a merchant or a caravaneer

*satya* — truth

*shravaka* — male lay follower of Jainism

*shravika* — female lay follower of Jainism

*shreyartham/shreyase* — for the spiritual merit of

*shudra* — a person of servile caste

*Shvetambara* — literally clad in white, one of the two main Jaina sects

*siddhachakra* — five supreme ones(arhat, siddha, acharya, upadhyaya & sadhu) worshipped collectively, by representing them on a plaque, along with four other essentials of the Jaina religion

| | |
|---|---|
| *stri-dhana* | the wealth of a woman given specifically to her for her own use |
| *strimoksha* | spiritual liberation of women |
| *sushravaka* | a good *shravaka* |
| *sushravika* | a good *shravika* |
| *suta* | a son |
| *sutaa* | a daughter |
| *tirtha* | literally a ford, a place of pilgrimage |
| *tirthankara* | the omniscient spiritual teachers of the Jainas; a synonym for *Jina* |
| *tri-tirthi* | an image showing figures of three *Jinas*, usually one of them is more prominent |
| *tunk* | top of a mountain or hill on which there is a shrine or several shrines |
| *vadhu* | daughter-in-law; wife |
| *vaishya* | a person of mercantile caste |
| *vamsha* | race, dynasty or family |
| *varna* | literally colour; used for four castes often as ritual statuses |
| *Vasudeva*, | also called as *Narayana*, is one of the five categories of Great Men in Jaina Puranas. There are in all 63 great men, 24 Tirthankaras, 12 Chakravartins, 9 Baladevas, 9 Vasudevas and 9 Prativasudevas. |

# Preface

As a schoolgirl, while reading history textbooks or even language books, I always searched for women figures but found very few. I felt odd but thought that I am the only one thinking that way and never talked to anybody about it. In my college days, in mid and late seventies, whenever the issues of women were discussed, I participated. By this time, I had become more aware of the gender inequality around me. However, this did not prompt me to do anything about it. My interest in women's issues was there lying dormant in my mind. I continued to lead a normative life, completed my masters in commerce and got married. Like all other women around me, took a secondary role in my family. Though, my married life was happy and peaceful, I got the first hand experience of the disadvantages of being a woman and of being a homemaker. The job of a homemaker, though important, is not valued in our society. Now, I was not satisfied with being just a homemaker and wanted to change the way I led my life. After many years, I discovered my interest in history and decided to restart my education. I did my M.A. in history and registered for Ph.D. deciding to do research in women's history. As, by now, I had also developed interest in epigraphy, with the help my guide Dr Shah, chose the present topic. This education, the second inning, was for me the real education, when I was doing something that I loved, not just following the beaten track.

The purpose of narrating my life story is that I consider myself as one of the representatives of average middle-class, middle-aged, educated Indian women. The churning of thoughts goes on in the mind but hardly a ripple is visible outside. It is not that someone is stopping them from doing or saying something but they do not dare to question the social norms. If this is the case with a woman from an educated family, holding liberal views, then how can we expect women from more disadvantaged sections to speak up?

Nevertheless, my journey from a homemaker to a researcher has been very educating and insightful. Now, as before, I note the women's problems, but unlike before, I also make an effort to analyse and understand them.

Of course in India, there have been women, more courageous and bold, who have chalked out careers for themselves, and have made a mark in the society. To mention two most prominent of them, India got its first woman prime minister way back in 1960's. Today, a woman holds the highest office of this country, that of the President of India. Women holding high posts are there in government departments, corporate world, educational institutions, and so on. However, in spite of the glaring achievements of a few women, many women are still discriminated against, exploited and oppressed. This happens because people (both, men and women) hold misogynist views. In order to change this we need to change the mindset of the people.

Religion plays a significant role in shaping the views of the people, and in the past, it played a major role. Most of the religions took superiority of men for granted. Patriarchy was, and still is, the norm. However, the nature and degree of patriarchy is region, religion and time specific. This is why women's experiences in different religious traditions are different, and even within the same religion, experiences of those belonging to different strata, places and times are different.

Jainism, like all other religions, was and still is a patriarchal religion. However, it adopted a liberal attitude towards women in certain respects. Nevertheless, did it practice what it preached? This book addresses the issue by taking the case of the Jainas of Gujarat. It also tries to locate modifications taking place in the patriarchal ideals during the period of study. It is an attempt to understand Jaina women's world-view, as far as possible, from their own sources.

Like all other religions, the Jainas have their *thirthas* or holy places, which they visit, in vast pilgrim bands called *sanghas*. Thousands of people from Gujarat, Rajasthan and other places visit these places. People visiting these places make donations in the form of images and other venerated objects. They also donate for the construction or renovation of the temples etc. Their donations are recorded mostly on the objects donated. These records, called as inscriptions or epigraphic records are the original sources used for the present research.

The five most important *thirthas* of the Jainas, known as *panchatirthas*, are: Shatrunjaya, Samet Sikhar or Mt. Parshvanatha, Arbuda or Abu, Girnar and Chandragiri. Of these, Shatrunjaya and Girnar are in Gujarat while Abu, though in Rajasthan, is just near the northern border of Gujarat. Inscriptions from these three places and many more find place in this book.

This research is based on the study of nearly 4500 inscriptions of men and women. Of these, nearly 550 are women's inscriptions. The time-period of these inscriptions is from 11th century to 19th century of the Common Era.

The inscriptional sources are preferred because they give a picture more close to reality than the textual sources. Of course, these sources have their own limitations, but considering that there are hardly any sources authored by women, women's inscriptions become all the more important.

The available literature on Jaina women is based mostly on textual sources, though some of them do consider inscriptional sources, albeit to a limited extent. More specifically, if the books on Gujarati Jaina women based on inscriptional sources are considered, there probably are hardly any. This book is a modest attempt to fill the gap.

# Acknowledgements

While I was doing research on this topic and later while I was trying to bring my thesis into the book form, I have received help and support from every corner. In this regard, I consider myself extremely fortunate. I would like to express my heartfelt gratitude to all those institutions and individuals who have helped me in the process.

This work was done under the supervision and guidance of Dr K.K. Shah, Professor and Head, P.G. Department of History, SNDT Women's University, Mumbai. His help support and guidance was available to me at every stage. In spite of numerous difficulties, personal problems and the pressure of work he patiently went through my notes on priority basis and gave valuable suggestions. I am deeply indebted to him and express my sincere thanks for his encouragement, support and guidance.

I came into contact with 'Jain Academy' through Prof Antarkar, Department of Philosophy, Mumbai University, at early phase of my work. The Jain Academy has greatly facilitated my work by giving me not only scholarship but constant encouragement and support. I am extremely thankful to both, Prof

Antarkar and the Jaina Academy, particularly Shri. C.N. Sanghavi, former Chairman and Trustee, Jaina Academy.

I express my sincere gratitude to:

Prof Jani, retired Prof and Head, Department of History, Saurashtra University, Rajkot for sending me the bibliography of relevant books.

Dr Rasesh Jamindar, Ahmedabad, who helped me by giving references of important source books.

Dr Nalini Joshi, Assistant Editor, Prakrit Kosha Vibhaga, Bandankar Oriental Research Institute, Pune, who made available to me her book on Jaina Women.

Mr A.W. Atre for helping me in translation of Sanskrit inscriptions, and

Mrs Ilaben Gajjar, my friend, for teaching and helping me in Gujarati from time to time.

Good libraries are the basic need of any research project. I have been benefited by the following libraries during my research work. I thank these institutions, trustees, and librarians for their help.

(a) Library of SNDT Women's University New Marine Lines, Mumbai.

(b) Asiatic Society of Mumbai, Mumbai-23

(c) Shri Mahavir Jaina Vidyalaya Library, Andheri, Mumbai.

(d) Shri Jaina Sahitya Mandal Pustakalaya, Irla, Mumbai.

(e) Forbes Gujarati Sabha, Mumbai.

(f) B.J. Institute of Learning and Research, Ahmedabad.

(g) Bhandarkar Oriental Reseaarch Institute, Pune.

(h) Deccan College Post Graduate and Research Institute, Pune.

I would especially like to express my gratitude to Ms. Minal Gandhi, former Assistant Librarian, SNDT Women's University Library, Mumbai, who has always been very helpful and considerate and to the Library staff.

For more than four years, I was associated with the PG Department of History, SNDT Women's University, Mumbai. During the period, I worked in a friendly and supportive atmosphere. The credit of this must go to the faculty members of this Department, Meherjyoti Sangle and Jaswandi Wamburkar Utagikar.

Work of writing thesis cannot be done without the blessings of the elders and support of the family and friends. My parents, Vijaykumar and Meena Paranjpay, as also my mother-in-law Malti Joshi have been a source of constant encouragement to me. I am indebted to my mother also for making a beautiful cover page in short span of time. She is an artist and though with age she is not keeping well, she gladly prepared the painting for the cover page. My sisters Mukta and Megha and members of my husband's family have also boosted my interest from time to time.

The support of your spouse is of utmost importance for any demanding activity. My husband Vijay, has not only supported, encouraged and motivated me but was as much involved in this work as I was. In spite of being very busy with his own work, he did everything right from helping me in my household cores to reading my manuscript and making useful suggestions and even proof reading. He guided me whenever I became directionless. My son Chaitanya and daughter-in-law Shruti helped me in all possible ways. The interest and curiosity of these three in my work resulted into several discussions and kept me energized and motivated.

I would like to thank Mr Madhukar and Mrs Meghana Deshpande for carefully doing the typing work.

In the end I express my gratitude to Rawat Publications, especially Mr. Pranit Rawat, who graciously accepted to publish this book. It is because of him that the book has seen the light of the day.

# 1

# Introduction

> Women and men have entered the historical process under different conditions and have passed through it at different rates of speed. If recording, defining, and interpreting the past marks man's entry into history, this occurred for males in the third millennium B.C. It occurred for women (and only some of them) with a few notable exceptions in the nineteenth century. Until then, all History was for women pre-History.
>
> —Gerda Lerner[1]

'Feminism', the word that we hear so often nowadays, is in reality an ideology. This ideology believes that women suffer from injustice on the basis of sex and that women's subordination is systematic. It also tries to give some explanation for this state of affairs and suggests the ways in which this situation could be changed.[2] The academic expression of 'feminism' is generally termed as 'women's studies'.[3] In the past thirty years the discipline of women's studies has made great progress. Many books have been written and numerous seminars and group discussions have been and are being organised on the issues of women. Various educational institutions have also started courses on women's studies. Today, books on women's studies occupy considerable space in libraries. All this has created a general awareness about the issues of women among at least some sections of the population. On the other hand, Indian society is still a patriarchal society. Not only men but even many women still firmly hold patriarchal values. TV channels and cinema too bombard stereotypical serials and movies on the people. Thus, there is a gap between the ideal and the actual.

Today, many women, especially the educated ones, who are exposed to feminism, have to live with a constant 'tug of war' between feminism and patriarchy in their minds. This experience suggests that perhaps the women in the past ages did not have to face this dilemma, because they were unaware of feminism. However, was it really so? What were the experiences of the women in the past about the world in which they lived? These and many such questions motivated me to take up research in the field of 'women's history', which is a part of women's studies and which, according to Gerda Lerner, is "an effort to reconstruct female past".[4]

Gerda Lerner feels that in order to arrive at universal history, we must first have women's history. In her words, "... women have always been making history, living it and shaping it. However, history of women has a special character, a built-in distortion: it comes to us refracted through the lens of men's observations; refracted again through values, which consider 'man' the measure. What we know of the experience of women has been transmitted to us largely through the reflections of men, how we see and interpret what we know about women has been shaped for us through a value system defined by men. And so, to construct a new history that will with true equality reflect the dual nature of humankind—its male and female aspect—we must first pause to reconstruct the missing half-the female experience: women's history".[5] In another place, she also says that gender must be added as an analytical category to history. Thus, when gender is considered with race, class, ethnicity etc., in analysing any given period or event, an entirely new dimension is added to social history.[6]

Gender, in its most recent usage, seems to have first appeared among American feminists, who wanted to insist on the fundamentally social quality of distinctions based on sex.[7] Since then the term 'gender has' been used by scholars in a variety of way's, ranging from theoretical positions to a simple descriptive reference to relation between sexes.[8]

In India too, feminist ideology has brought a change in the historiography on women, which previously had followed a set pattern since the colonial days. Women were treated as passive objects, who were acted upon. Their men granted a particular status to them and this status was treated as an index of civilisation. If the men gave more freedom to women, they were supposed to be more civilised and vice versa. While writing women's history, women's thoughts and experiences were not necessarily considered. This was the paradigm created by Altekar's work, *Position of Women in Hindu Civilization: From Prehistoric Times to the Present Day,*[9] Altekar's work rooted, as it was in the nationalist ideology, was a product of the colonial mindset. However this work, though limiting and biased, is the best that is available to us by way of women's studies and continues to influence the historical writing on women.[10]

One of the first Indian scholars to challenge the Altekarian paradigm was Uma Chakravarti. According to her, the picture of the idyllic condition of women in Vedic age created by Altekar now pervades the collective consciousness of the upper castes in India, and has virtually crippled the emergence of a more analytically rigorous study of gender relations in ancient India.[11] In another article, Uma Chakravarti along with Kumkum Roy, reiterates the importance of gender as a category of historical analysis.[12]

The main purpose of this research is to study women from the gender perspective, taking into account, as far as possible, their own experiences. Societies generally distinguish between males and females and ascribe to them roles suitable to their sexes. This converts males into 'men' and females into 'women'. There are set norms, which govern the relationship between men and women. These norms vary according to time and space. It is in this sense that the term 'gender relations' has been used in this work. As society consists of both men and women, study of one to the exclusion of the other may give a distorted picture, and therefore, though the objective of this research is to make women visible, men also find place in it.

The gender identity is compounded and internally differentiated by social, political,[13] and also geographical and religious identities. The scope of this research, therefore, is limited to the Shvetambara Jainas of Gujarat.

## II

Jainism, along with Buddhism, represents the Shramanic tradition of Indian culture. It is an ancient religion, which challenged the Vedic religion. It was against the Vedic ritualism, animal sacrifices in *yajnas*, the birth-based caste system and the infallibility of Vedas. It also adopted a liberal attitude towards women.

On certain counts Jaina women were better placed than their Hindu sisters. Firstly, Jaina women were permitted to opt out of family life and renounce the world to become nuns. Secondly, Jainas gave considerable property rights to women. Thirdly, Jainism did not prescribe the practice of *sati*, and fourthly, the four-fold Jaina society consisted of *sadhus, sadhvis, shravakas* and *shravikas*. In this scheme women had a place of their own, though secondary, as *sadhvis* and *shravikas*, whereas the Brahmanical four-fold society consisted of *brahmans, kshatriyas, vaishyas* and *shudras*. Women as well as men belonged to the *vrarna* of their father, and women did not have a separate place of their own in this scheme. However, to what extent this liberal attitude was practised has to be verified.

Though Jainas have been a microscopic minority of the total Indian population, in several parts like Gujarat, Rajasthan and Karnataka, they are quite numerous as well as influential. Normally, they have been a business community and so because of their wealth their influence is much greater and stronger than warranted by their numbers.

According to Jaina tradition, Gujarat was the stronghold of Jainism from the remote antiquity. Rishabhadeva, the first *tirthankara,* performed penance at Shatrunjaya and Neminatha on Girnara,[14] but there is no archaeological evidence to support this. It is possible that the first wave of Jainism passed over Gujarat when Bhadrabahu went to the south in the 4th century B.C.E. Definite evidence of its existence is available from the Kshatrapa period. We find the use of Jaina technical terms like *kevalajnana* etc. in the inscription of Jayadamana (*E.I.* Vol. 6, p. 239). There are also archaeological evidences to confirm this view. The Bawa Pyara caves at Junagadh seem to be Jaina. Existence of similar early settlements in other parts of Saurashtra is attested by sculptures at Dhank. For the early medieval period, there are epigraphs in which two Gurjara kings use titles such as Vitaraga and Prashantaraga, almost exclusively applied to Jaina *tirthankaras* and may have been bestowed on or adopted by the kings themselves[15] (*E.I.* II, pp. 20–21). In the 5th century of Common Era a conference of Jaina monks was held in Vallabhi, Gujarat. This implies that it was a place convenient to many Jaina monks who did not use vehicle,[16] It could therefore be inferred that Jainism was prevalent in Gujarat since at least the early centuries of Common Era.

Jainism received little attention from the early Indologists. In fact, because of the similarities between Jainism and Buddhism, for long Jainism was thought to be a branch of Buddhism. The credit of removing this misconception goes to two German scholars Jacobi and George Buhler.[17] Since then, the scholars have taken profound interest in Jainism. Initially interest was limited to Jaina canon and philosophy but gradually it extended to sociology, history, art and architecture. Today, a great number of studies have been devoted to various aspects of Jaina society.

Jaina sources have also been used to write the social history of India. Some such works are: *Jainism in North India* (1932) by C.J. Shah,[18] *Life in Ancient India as Depicted in Jaina Canons* (1947)[19] and *Jaina Way of Life,*[20] both by J.C. Jain. All these books devote a few pages to women. *Ideal, Ideology and Practices: Studies in Jainism* (1987) edited by N.K. Singhi[21] is an anthology of essays on various aspects of Jainism. It contains two chapters on women, one by Vilas Sangave and another by the editor himself.

By far the most exhaustive work on the nature and structure of Jaina religion comes from the pen of Vilas Sangave. In the book, *Jain Community: A Social Survey*[22] the author has surveyed the Jaina religion and society right from the ancient period up to the modern times. He devotes one chapter to 'Marriage and Position of Women', in which the position of women, seen mainly in the context of the family and the social, religious, political and legal position, is studied. The author has compared the position of Jaina women with that of the Hindu women and concludes that the social and political status of Jaina and Hindu women was alike. However, in respect of the religious and legal position, Jaina women were better placed than their Hindu sisters were. However, Sangave has not used Jaina epigraphy as a source for his study.

S.B. Deo has used epigraphic as well as literary sources in his book, *History of Jain Monachism.*[23] In this book, as the title suggests, the author has dealt with the way of life of the Jaina ascetics. One full chapter has been devoted to the order of nuns. However, Jaina *shravakas* and *shravikas* do not form the subject of the author's research. *Gender & Salvation,*[24] which comes from the pen of Padmanabh S. Jaini, is a survey of the works by Jaina *acharyas*, on the topic of *strimoksha*. In this volume, the author brings to light the text which were until then untranslated, evidencing a centuries old debate between the two principal Jaina sects, the Digambaras and the Shvetambaras, on the critical issue of whether or not women can attain spiritual liberation. This book is very valuable and important. However, in this book 'women' form the subject of the debate and not of the of study.

There are also a few books in existence, which are devoted exclusively to Jaina women. A Hindi book, *Jaina Jagat ki Mahilayem,*[25] by Pyarachandji Maharaj was published in 1949. It contains the stories of the famous women of the Jaina tradition, most of whom are mythical. Yet another Hindi book *Jaina Dharma ki Pramukh Sadhviyam evam Mahilayem*[26] is by Hirabai Boradia. It was originally a Ph.D. thesis of Indore University (1975). It contains short biographies of learned Jaina women and nuns, from tradition as well as history. At certain places she has used inscriptions as evidences. Two more books, *Jaina Agama me Nari*[27] and *Jaina Agamat Stri,*[28] the first in Hindi and the other in Marathi, focus on Jaina woman. Both of them base their study on the Jaina canons and do not use epigraphy as their source. *The Unknown Pilgrims*[29] is a very scholarly book by N. Shanta. The author has used all kinds of sources—scriptures, ancient texts, biographies, epigraphy and also iconography to study the life of Jaina women ascetics, both historical as well as contemporary, belonging to both the sects, Shvetambara as well as Digambara. The *shravikas* or the lay Jaina woman do not find place in this book. In the essay, 'Women and Jainism in India',[30] the author Balbir Nalini too studies both Digambara and Shvetambara Jaina women of the past as well as of the present. She does not restrict herself to the *sadhvis* alone but includes *shravikas* also in her study. The essay is however mostly based on the textual sources.

P.V. Research Institute, Varanasi, published a list of doctoral dissertations in Jainism and Buddhism[31] in 1983. However, it does not contain any work on Jaina women based on epigraphical sources. Furthermore, I have not come across any such work published in little more than a couple of decades after 1983 either.

## III

This study belongs to the class of regional history, and the region with which the study is concerned is that of Gujarat. The modern state of Gujarat was formed in 1960. Earlier, in the past, the boundaries of Gujarat, like those of other kingdoms of the time, were always shifting. Before the Solanki rule, different parts of Gujarat were known by different names. South Gujarat was known as Lata, North Gujarat and part of west Gujarat was known as Anartta and Saurashtra was known as Surashtra.[32] Under the Solankis the present Gujarat came to be called by the name of Gurjara-mandala, because for the first time the rulers identified themselves with the land over which they ruled. Though they might be outsiders they lived here and tried their best to encourage art, literature, trade and commerce. With the royal patronage and private enterprise, the country flourished as never before and acquired cultural and political unity. This was expressed by the word Gujarat or Gurjara-mandala.[33] For the purpose of the present study, the term 'Gujarat' includes the whole of the present state of Gujarat as well as a few more places located in south Rajasthan. These places, though located in Rajasthan, are culturally akin to Gujarat and have a considerable Jaina population. Abu though situated in south Rajasthan, is one of the most important pilgrim centres of Jainas.

The British took keen interest in the history of Gujarat. One of the first historians of Gujarat was James Bird, who wrote *History of Gujarat*[34] in 1835. H.G. Briggs wrote *The Cities of Gujarashtra*[35] in 1849. Another famous historian of Gujarat, who wrote in English, was M.S. Commissariat. His two-volume work *A History of Gujarat*, still remains useful to the students of history.[36] S.B. Rajyagor's work *History of Gujarat* was published in 1982.[37] It is an extensive survey of the history of Gujarat right from the pre-historical times up to the modern period. The emphasis of the study is on political history and the author has used literary as well as non-literary sources for the study. However women find only a passing reference in it.

Among the authors who wrote in Gujarati, mention may be made of Durgashankar Kevalram Shastri, who wrote—*Gujaratno Madhyakalina Rajaputa Itihas*, (Vols. I and II)[38] and H.G. Shastri—*Gujaratno Prachina Itihas*.[39]

In almost in all the above books, women get very little space. There is only one book that is solely devoted to the women of Gujarat—*Gujarat ni Nari* by Elaben Bhatt.[40] This book contains an account of Gujarati women, right from the Puranic times up to the present, and is mainly based on the literary sources.

## IV

The importance of epigraphy for the writing of history can hardly be overemphasised. Epigraphy is the study of inscriptions and inscriptions literally mean any writing engraved on some object. Epigraphic records are of two types: one, engraved on behalf of the rulers and the other, incised on behalf of private individuals or organisations. Most of these inscriptions record donations made in favour of religious establishments or installations of images for worship.[41] In India, the beginning of epigraphical studies can be traced back to the end of the 18th century. There are some indirect evidences, and that too of uncertain nature, to claim that in medieval India there were learned people who could decipher ancient inscriptions.[42] Nevertheless, the fact that early inscriptions, by and large, had become unintelligible to Indians themselves is proved by the failure of Firoz Shah Tuglaque, the Sultan of Delhi (1351–88), to have Ashokan pillars brought and set up in Delhi to be deciphered by the indigenous scholars.[43]

The golden era of Indian epigraphical research was inaugurated by James Princep, an officer of the mint at Calcutta, who successfully deciphered the earliest Brahmi inscriptions in 1836.[44] The job of editing and interpreting the inscriptions was undertaken with deep interest by many European scholars like G. Buhler, E. Senart, F. Kielhorn, E. Hultzsch, L. Rice, J.F. Fleet and others. The Indian scholars, who contributed immensely to the epigraphical studies include, amongst others, Bhagvanlal Indraji, R.L. Mitra, R.G. Bhandarkar, R.D. Banerji, D.R. Bhandarkar, D.C. Sircar. It is on the shoulders of these pioneers that 'Indian epigraphical studies' stands today.

In the beginning, inscriptions were mainly used for reconstructing political history of ancient and medieval India. Gradually, it began to be used for writing religious, cultural and other histories. Some efforts have also been made for writing women's history by using inscriptions as source. Prominent among them are Kumkum Roy, Leslee Orr and K.K. Shah. Kumkum Roy,[45] who in her study of inscriptions of Sanchi, found that the donors were nearly equally divided along gender lines, and that the women had a fair degree of control over their economic resources. Leslee Orr[46] has studied the Hindu, Jaina and Buddhist inscriptions of Tamil Nadu of the period between 8th century to 17th century, and found that women actively donated to the religious establishments, and that they were far from marginal. K.K. Shah's[47] book is an important contribution to the epigraphical studies on women. It gives alternative framework to the Altekarian one. Dealing with the women in ancient India, the author makes a powerful argument for revising the conventional historiography that perceives women as silent voices of history because they have little or nothing to do with the creation of its sources. The book draws on epigraphic accounts where women speak for themselves.

In the present work on Jaina women, inscriptions have been used as the main source for understanding gender relations among the Jainas of Gujarat. The preference for the epigraphic sources is on account of the fact that they give us a picture more close to reality than the textual sources. The information, which they can give us, may be limited in terms of the content but as far as the authenticity is concerned, they are most reliable. In any given society, people like to put into writing something that is accepted and respected by the society. Thus, they represent the norms and conventions followed by that society. However, there are also some such inscriptions which do not really fit into the norms, depicting deviations and variations from the norms. Therefore, epigraphic sources reflect norms as well as variations or, in some cases, deviations from the norms. Such inscriptions represent those people who, in a sense, challenge the norms. Another important reason for preferring inscriptional sources is the paucity of other sources authored by women. For the medieval period, there are very few sources authored by women in general and Jaina women in particular. In such a situation inscriptions appear to articulate some of the voices. Inscriptions in which women figure as the main donors can be taken to represent the women's world view. This is not to say that such inscriptions were drafted by women, but as K.K. Shah put it, "Our assumption that women have articulated themselves in inscriptions is based on the argument that the attributes of identity along with names must have been offered by the women themselves".[48] Furthermore, the women donors must have also provided the names of those persons for whose merit they were making the donation.

## V

Gujarat is very rich in epigraphic sources. The bibliography of the inscriptions of Gujarat published by Gujarat Itihas Parishad in several parts during 1962–72, enlists (i) 439 Prakrit-Sanskrit inscriptions on stone and copper plates as well as 668 image inscriptions dated up to 1300 C.E., (ii) 443 Sanskrit, Sanskrit-Gujarati and Gujarati inscriptions on stone and copperplates, dated from 1301 to 1760 C.E., (iii) 3,695 image inscriptions dated from 1301 to 1760 C.E., and (iv) 623 Arabic and Persian inscriptions dated from 920 to 1953 C.E.[49] Thus, the total number of published inscriptions up to 1972 was 5,868. If the number of inscriptions lying unpublished or published subsequently is added, the number would increase immensely. Out of these 5,868 inscriptions, an overwhelming majority are Jaina inscriptions. It is clear, therefore, that there is great scope for using epigraphic sources for studying various aspects of Jainism in Gujarat.

The study of inscriptions on modern lines commenced in Gujarat during the first half of the 19th century. Since then numerous inscriptions in Gujarat have been published in various journals and books.

Epigraphic records have been a very valuable source of information for the political and cultural history of Gujarat. Right from Bhagvanlal Indraji[50] and A.K. Forbes, the author of *Rasmal* (1924),[51] almost all historians have availed themselves of this valuable source, especially for studying the ancient period. While discussing the epigraphical studies in Gujarat, the name that comes immediately to one's mind is that of H.D. Sankalia. He has truly enriched this field. Two of his important works are *The Archaeology of Gujarat*[52] and *The Studies in Historical and Cultural Geography and Ethnography of Gujarat*.[53] Sankalia has used epigraphic, archaeological and architectural sources for writing the cultural, religious and political history of Gujarat in the first book. In the second, he uses epigraphic sources to trace the origin and development of place names, and various castes as well as personal names. The eminent epigraphist of Gujarat, H.G. Shastri has written several books on various aspects of the history of Gujarat. In his book, *The Historical and Cultural Study of the Inscriptions of Gujarat*,[54] he has used epigraphic sources to study the political, religious literary and architectural aspects of Gujarat up to 1304 A.D. Two other scholars who have contributed to the field are Rasesh Jamindar and Ramlal Parikh.[55] All the above-mentioned scholars and many more have used inscriptions as sources to enrich Gujarat history. However, I have not yet come across any work in which epigraphical sources have been used for a study on the women of Gujarat. This study is, therefore, an effort in that direction.

## VI

As has been mentioned earlier, this research will try to make Jaina women of Gujarat visible by using epigraphic sources. For this purpose many standard journals like, *Indian Antiquary*, *Epigraphia Indica* and *Corpus Inscriptinum Indicarum*, etc. are available. There are also some books, mostly in Gujarati, in which Jaina inscriptions of Gujarat have been compiled. These books, more than the standard English journals on epigraphy, seem to be of greater importance for this study and therefore have been used as primary sources. The main source books which have been used in this work are:

1. *Prachina Jaina Lekha Sangraha,* part-II (*PJLS*).
2. *Jaina Dhatu Pratima Lekha Sangraha*, part-I (*JDLS-I*).
3. *Jaina Dhatu Pratima Lekha Sangraha*, part-II (*JDLS-II*).
4. *Prachina Lekh Sangraha* part-I (*PLS*).
5. *Shri Arbuda Prachina Jaina Lekha Sandoha* (Abu part-II) (*APJLS*).
6. *Shri Jaina Pratima Lekha Sangraha* (*JPLS*).
7. *Shri Radhanapura Pratima Lekh Sandoha* (*RPLS*).
8. *Shri Shatrunjaya Giriraja Darshana ane Shilpa Sthapatya kalamam Shatrunjaya* (*Shat*).
9. *Nirgrantha,* Vol. III (*Nir*).

The first of these books contains Jaina inscriptions, mainly of western India, and are related to Shvetambaras. It contains copper plate inscriptions, stone inscriptions and stone image inscriptions, but not metal image inscriptions. The total number of inscriptions in this volume are 557. Inscriptions from Shatrunjaya, Girinara, Abu and many other places from Gujarat and Rajasthan find place in this book. Of these, those from Gujarat and Abu have been utilised. The oldest inscription of this collection is dated V.S. 996 and the latest is dated V.S. 1903.

*JDLS,* Part I and II together contain more than 2500 inscriptions from sixty-six places of Gujarat and Rajasthan.

*PLS-I* contains nearly 500 inscriptions, all metal image inscriptions, mostly from Gujarat and Rajasthan. Of these, those belonging to Gujarat have been included in this study.

In *APJLS* 664 inscriptions of Abu have been compiled. These also include 208 inscriptions already published in *PJLS*.

Majority of the inscriptions compiled in *JPLS* are from Tharad—district Banasakantha. It also contains inscriptions from other cities and villages from north Gujarat and south Rajasthan.

*RPLS* contains nearly 500 inscriptions from one single place, Radhanpur, which is a Jaina pilgrim centre of Gujarat.

In *Shat,* another set of nearly 500 inscriptions from Shatrunjay, the biggest and very ancient pilgrim centre of the Jainas, have been compiled. However, we do not find many old inscriptions at this place. Because of the repair work that is undertaken over here from time to time, many old inscriptions have been destroyed or whitewashed. Rivalry between the sects is also one of the reasons of the destruction of the old inscriptions.[56]

A few inscriptions published recently in the journal *Nirgrantha* also find place in this study.

Most of the Jaina inscriptions are donative in nature. Donations could be in the form of grant of land, providing for the construction of the temple, installation of image, providing for the *puja* of the *tirthankaras* and so on.

In Gujarat, worship of Parshvanatha was most popular. Next to him were Shantinatha, Mahavira, Rishabhadeva, Neminatha, Ajitanatha and Chandraprabha in descending order. In addition to the twenty-four *tirthankaras*, there are also images of Ambika,

Saraswati, Chakreshwari, Gautamsvami, Kapardi Yaksha and Simandharasvami. There are also a few *chaturvinshatipattas.* Sometimes, the donors also installed the images of themselves and their relatives in the temples built by them. For instance, ministers Vastupala and Tejapala installed the images of their ancestors, themselves and their descendants in the temples built by them. Among the *tirthankaras,* Rishabhadeva was especially associated with the *mahatirtha* of Shatrunjaya, and Neminatha with that of Ujjayanta (Girnar). Mahavira was associated with the *tirtha* of Satyapura (Sanchor in Rajasthan).[57]

Among the Jainas, the contributions of *Jina bhavana, Jina bimba* and *Jina puja* were regarded as meritorious. The main aim of donations was the *shreyas* (spiritual bliss/merit) of oneself and of one's relatives.[58]

Nearly 5,000 inscriptions belonging to Gujarat and adjoining parts of Rajasthan have been collected for the present study. Leaving aside some incomplete inscriptions and some unrelated inscriptions, more than 4,400 inscriptions dated between 11th century and 19th century have been analysed. However, inscriptions, particularly of women, belonging to the earlier period that is the period prior to the 11th century are very few. Most of the inscriptions, except a few royal or ministerial ones, are quite brief. They record particulars about donors, the monks who installed the images, the person for whose merit the donations were made and the date. Many women find mention in these inscriptions, not only as relatives of the male donors but as donors themselves. They thus provide us with very useful data for studying women from the gender perspective.

## VII

Traditionally, Indian history has been divided into three parts, namely, ancient history, medieval history and modern history, corresponding to Hindu, Muslim and British rulers respectively. This periodisation is based on some major political events, in which mostly men were involved. Though these changes did affect women in certain ways, yet this periodisation does not seem useful for the study of women.

For Jaina history, R. Williams[59] has suggested the following periodisation:

1. The early period (6th c. B.C. E.–4th c. C.E.)—the dark age, covering the first millennium, belonging to the whole of Shvetambara canon and such fundamental Digambara works as the *Prabhrtas* of Kundakunda and the *Tattvartha-su-tra*.
2. The medieval period, extending from the 5th century to the end of the 13th century, is the most important historically and sees the greatest achievements in art and literature. In this period, Jaina groups in various parts of western and southern India were found exerting influence on the political developments of the time.
3. 14th century is the great divide. The expansion of Islam and renaissance of Shaivism in the south shattered the flourishing Jaina communities. From then on Jainism was on the defensive. This modern period is, therefore, by comparison with the past, an age of decadence.

These major changes must have also affected the lives of women in some way or the other.

Sagarmal Jain[60] in his study on Jaina women, has suggested yet another periodisation:

1. Period prior to sixth century B.C.E.
2. From 6th century B.C.E. up to the beginning of 5th century C.E. (Age of Canons).
3. From 5th century C.E. up to the beginning of 8th century C.E. (Age of Prakrit commentaries).
4. From 8th century up to the beginning of 12th century C.E. (Age of Sanskrit commentaries).

Sagarmal Jain has based his work on the religious literary sources, for which this periodisation seems useful.

On the other hand, Hirabai Boradiya,[61] whose book is also on the Jaina women and is based on literary sources, uses a slightly different periodisation:

1. Jaina *sadhvis* and learned women of the pre-historic period.

2. Jaina *sadhvis* and learned women, contemporary to Mahavira.
3. Jaina *sadhvis* and learned women of post-Mahavira period.
4. Jaina *sadhvis* and women belonging to the period—first century C.E. to seventh century C.E.
5. Jaina *sadhvis* and learned women belonging to the period—eighth century to fifteenth century C.E.
6. Jaina *sadhvis* and learned women belonging to the period—sixteenth century to eighteenth century C.E.

The present study is based on the inscriptional sources. On arranging the inscriptions chronologically and classifying them a pattern has been noted. The scheme of periodisation for this study is based on this pattern.

The inscriptions have been classified into the following categories:

1. Man: The inscriptions in which a man is the donor.
2. Men: The inscriptions in which two or more men are the donors.
3. G-Man: The inscriptions recording donations by a group of men and women but where a man is the chief donor.
4. Woman: The inscriptions in which a woman is the donor.
5. Women: The inscriptions in which two or more women are the donors.
6. G-Woman: The inscriptions recording donations by a group of men and women but where a woman is the chief donor.
7. Family: the inscriptions recording donations by group of men and women but where the chief donor is not mentioned.

These categories can be grouped in two ways: one, by including group donations headed by a man (G-Man) in men's and group donations headed by a woman (G-Woman) into women's inscriptions, and two, by including both, G-Man and G-Woman inscriptions in the third group named as 'Group Donations'.

**Table 1**

*Jaina Inscriptions of Gujarat: A Break up*

| | *Century > (C.E.)* | *11th* | *12th* | *13th* | | *14th* | *15th* | *16th* | *17th* | *18th* | *19th* | *Total* |
|---|---|---|---|---|---|---|---|---|---|---|---|---|
| | | | | *V&T ** | *NON-V&T* | | | | | | | |
| 1. | Man | 15 | 69 | 44 | 232 | 291 | 574 | 116 | 71 | 44 | 43 | 1499 |
| 2. | Men | 1 | 14 | 3 | 38 | 91 | 235 | 46 | 23 | 13 | 11 | 475 |
| 3. | G-man | | 5 | | 11 | 20 | 996 | 220 | 50 | 10 | 4 | 1316 |
| 4. | Woman | 2 | 19 | | 19 | 27 | 205 | 62 | 36 | 28 | 22 | 420 |
| 5. | Women | | 3 | | | 2 | 4 | 1 | 5 | 3 | 1 | 19 |
| 6. | G-woman | | 1 | | 2 | | 76 | 32 | 7 | 2 | | 120 |
| 7. | Family | 1 | 6 | | 8 | 21 | 135 | 73 | 19 | 6 | 6 | 275 |
| 8. | Others | 5 | 19 | | 19 | 26 | 58 | 70 | 40 | 34 | 36 | 307 |
| 9. | Total | 24 | 136 | 47 | 329 | 478 | 2283 | 620 | 251 | 140 | 123 | 4431 |
| 10. | % of Group Donations (3+6+7) | 4 | 9 | 0 | 6 | 9 | 53 | 52 | 30 | 13 | 8 | |
| 11. | % of Women Donors (4+5+6) | 8 | 17 | 0 | 6 | 6 | 12 | 15 | 19 | 24 | 19 | |

* *The inscriptions of the 13th century have been sub-divided into V&T and Non-V&T. V&T stands for Vastupala and Tejapala.*

According to the first:

1. Men's inscriptions: (Man + Men + G-Man)
2. Women's inscriptions: (Woman + Women + G-Women)
3. Family donations

This type of grouping helps us to ascertain the actual number and percentage of women donors.

According to the second:

1. Men's inscriptions (Man + Men)
2. Women's inscriptions (Woman + Women)
3. Group inscriptions (G-Man+ G-Woman+ Family)

This type of grouping shows us the tendency of men and women to come together for specific purposes like donating for religious purpose.

Referring to the Table 1 which shows all the above categories and groups, we note firstly, that the percentage of women's inscriptions (according to the first way of grouping) fluctuates over the centuries; however, overall it shows a rising trend (with the exception of 12th century). Secondly, the percentage of group donations (according the second way of grouping) is less than 10 up to 14th century. However, the same shoots up to more than 50 in the 15th and 16th centuries. In the 17th century also it is as high as 30 and again drops down below 13 for the 18th and 19th centuries. This indicates that during 15th, 16th and 17th centuries, group donations were very popular. Men and women frequently came together to donate. This fact seems important from the point of view of gender relations. All these factors have been considered while developing the scheme of periodisation:

| | |
|---|---|
| Period I | 11th c.–14th c. |
| Period II | 15th c.–17th c. |
| Period III | 18th and 19th centuries |

## VIII

Personal identity as a concept, in terms of one's social self, was first used by K.K. Shah. Evolving the appropriate conceptual framework and methodology to collect, classify and analyse epigraphic data, he laid down the cardinal principle that when donors figure with multiple attributes of identity, chronology of attributes in construction of identity is the key to the self perception of the persons concerned and would be of deeper significance to develop an understanding of pattern rather than frequency.[62] While putting his/her identity in a public record, in most cases, a person chooses the attributes of identity carefully. He/she either goes by the norms of the society (social construction of identity) or by the self-perception, or both. This concept of personal identity has been used for analysing the inscriptions.

The discussion on patriarchy becomes inevitable while discussing gender relations. The word 'patriarchy', as defined by the *World Book Dictionary,* means: a form of social organization in which the father is the head of the family and in which descent is reckoned in the male line, the children belong to the father's clan. The joint family of Hindus and Roman family are the examples".[63]

Patriarchy, as a concept, has been used in different ways. Weber in 1947 used it to refer to a system of government in which men ruled societies through their position as heads of households. This usage included domination of both younger males and all females.[64]

"The meaning of the term has evolved since Weber, especially in writings by radical feminists who developed the element of domination of women by men and who paid less attention to the issue of how men dominated each other, and by dual system theorists, who have sought to develop a concept and theory of patriarchy as a system which exists along side capitalism".[65]

Sylvia Walby defines patriarchy as "a system of social structures in which men dominate, oppress and exploit women",[66] whereas Maithreyi Krishnaraj uses it to denote the structural system of male domination.[67]

If patriarchy is defined as the structures, practices and beliefs of male domination, then in the Indian context, patriarchal joint family is one such structure of male domination. Some of the beliefs and practices associated with the Indian patriarchy are:

1. Women are considered inferior to men.
2. There is segregation of public and private spheres and domestic activities are considered to be women's domain while public activities are regarded as men's job.
3. Dependence of women on their male relatives is advocated, and to a great extent their freedom to act is curtailed.
4. Girls are married young and widow-remarriage is not approved of but widower-remarriage is accepted.
5. Polygamy exists.
6. Women identify themselves with reference to their male guardians.

However, the strictness with which these and other such norms are followed is not the same always. In other words, the degree of patriarchy varies with time and space. Besides, patriarchy may not be applied in the same measures to all aspects of life. If in a particular society the degree of patriarchy is less, women get more space and vice versa.

The present effort tries to find out how much space was available to the Gujarati Jaina women within patriarchal framework, i.e., whether the patriarchal norms were strictly followed or were flexible enough to allow women some freedom and agency.

## IX

In an effort to analyse the inscriptions from a gender perspective, three questions were addressed to the inscriptions: (i) who were the persons forming the identity of the donor, (ii) who were the persons for whose religious merit the donation was made by the donor, and (iii) what were the objects donated.

Both the way the donor identifies himself/herself and the way the donor chooses the person on whom the benefit of donation is to be conferred are governed by the social norms, and in this case by patriarchy. Therefore, the answers to the first two questions help us to find out the extent to which patriarchy has a hold on the donor, while the objects donated give us some idea about the financial resources, which were at the disposal of the person. Information on some other aspects like the caste to which the donor belonged, has also been collected. From the above information, a pattern of women's inscriptions is arrived at. The scope of this work is limited to the study of women's inscriptions. However, in order to have a comparative perspective, men's inscriptions have also been studied and some observations made about the same, though these have not been thoroughly analysed like the women's inscriptions. Based on these observations the pattern of men's inscriptions is arrived at. Subsequently, the two patterns are compared.

Monks and nuns are also a part of the four-fold Jaina society. In most of the inscriptions *sadhus,* that is monks, find mention as the motivators, *gurus* or the consecrators of the images, whereas the *sadhvis*, that is, nuns, find mention very rarely. From these references to monks and nuns, the study will try to throw some light on the position of nuns vis-à-vis monks.

It has been noted that most of the women used their familial attributes of identity. The other attributes of identity used by them were caste, the place of residence, professional attribute and the religious attribute *shravika.* However, generally the caste or place of residence formed a part of their husbands'/fathers' identity. The professional attributes used by the women were also, in most cases, the feminine forms of the male professional attributes. The religious attribute *shravika* was their very own attribute. Thus, the familial attribute and the religious attribute were the two most important attributes of a Jaina woman's identity. Nevertheless, only some women used the religious attribute. The Jaina women located themselves mainly within the familial framework. Keeping this in mind, women's inscriptions have been classified in all the chapters.

The second chapter of this work will deal with analysis of inscriptions from the 11th century to 14th centuries of the present era. The third chapter will deal with the analysis of the inscriptions of 15th, 16th and 17th centuries of the present era, and the fourth chapter will cover the analysis of the inscriptions belonging to the 18th and 19th centuries. Out of more than four thousand inscriptions, which have been studied, translations of the summarised contents of some inscriptions have been included in each of these three chapters. These inscriptions are dated in Vikram era or Vikram samvat (V.S.). The mutilated portions of these inscriptions, as indicated in the sources, have been shown by the dots (...), while dashes (---) have been used to indicate those parts of the inscriptions, which have been found unrelated to this study and therefore have been omitted.

In the fifth chapter, the findings of this analysis will be compared with the literary sources and the last chapter will be the concluding chapter.

Thus, this research intends to see whether the liberal attitude adopted by Jainas towards women was practised or not, how much space was available to women within the patriarchal framework, and to throw some light on the gender relations in the Jaina community of Gujarat.

## Notes

1. Gerda Lerner, *The Creation of Patriarchy* (New York: OUP, 1986), p. 226.
2. Preeti Karmarkar, *Feminist Theory and Knowledge* (Pune: Women's Study Centre, University of Pune, 1998), p. 3.
3. K.K. Shah, *The Problem of Identity: Women in Early Indian Inscriptions* (Delhi: OUP, 2001), p. 5.
4. Gerda Lerner, *Majority Finds its Past* (New York: OUP, 1979), p. 168.
5. Ibid., p. 160.
6. Ibid., p. 172.
7. Joan Wallach Scott, "Gender a Useful Category of Historical Analysis" in Joan Wallach Scott (ed.), *Feminism and History* (New York: OUP, 1996), p. 153.
8. Ibid., p. 154.
9. A.S. Altekar, *The Position of Women in Hindu Civilization*, 3rd edition (Delhi: Motilal Banarasidas, 1962).

10. Uma Chakravarti, "Beyond the Altekarian Paradigm" in Kumkum Roy (ed.), *Women in Early Indian Societies* (New Delhi: Manohar, 1999), p. 77.
11. Ibid., p. 80.
12. Kumkum Roy and Uma Chakravarti, "In Search of Our Past: A Review of the Limitations and Possibilities of the Historiography of Women in Early India", in *EPW*, 30 April, 1988, p. WS-9.
13. Joan Wallach Scott, "Introduction", in self-edited *Feminism and History* (New York: OUP, 1996), p. 7.
14. C.B. Sheth, *Jainism in Gujarat* (Bombay: Shri Vijaydevasur Sangh Gyan Samiti, 1953), p. VI.
15. H.D. Sankalia, *Archaeology of Gujarat,* 1st edition (Bombay: Natwarlal & Co., 1941), pp. 233–34.
16. C.B. Sheth, op. cit.
17. S. Gopalan, *Outlines of Jainism* (New Delhi: Wiley Eastern Pvt. Ltd., 1973), p. 2.
18. C.J. Shah, *Jainism in North India* (London: Longman & Green Co., 1932).
19. J.C. Jain, *Life in Ancient India: As Depicted in Jaina Canons* (Bombay: New Book Company, 1965).
20. J.C. Jain, *Jain Way of Life*, 1st edition (Gurgaon: The Academic Press, 1991).
21. N.K. Singhi, *Ideal, Ideology and Practices: Studies in Jainism* (Jaipur: Printwell Publishers, 1987).
22. Vilas Adinath Sangave, *Jain a Community: A Social Survey* (Bombay: Popular, 1959).
23. S.B. Deo, *History of Jaina Monachism from Inscriptions and Literature* (Poona: Deccan College, 1956).
24. Padmanabh S. Jaini, *Gender and Salvation*, 1st Indian edition (New Delhi: Munshiram Manoharlal, 1992).
25. Shri. Pyarachandji Maharaj, *Jaina Jagata ki Mahilayem* (Ratlam: Shri Jainodaya Pustaka Prakashan Samiti, 1949).
26. Hirabai Boradia, *Jaina Dharma ki Pramukha Sadhviym evam Mahilayem* (Varanasi: P.V. Research Institute, 1991).
27. Komal Jain, *Jaina Agama men Nari*, (ed.) Ghanashyamdas Mukhia (Indore: 1986).

28. Nalini Joshi, *Jaina Agamat Stri* (Pune: K.K. Jain, 2000).
29. N. Shanta, *The Unknown Pilgrims: The Voice of Sadhvis,* 1st English edition (Delhi: Shri Satguru Publications, 1997).
30. Nalini Balbir, "Women and Jainism in India" in Arvind Sharma (ed.), *Women in Indian Religions* (Delhi: OUP, 2002).
31. Sagarmal Jain and A.P. Singh, *Doctoral Dissertations in Jaina and Buddhist Studies* (Varanasi: P.V. Research Institute, 1983).
32. H.D. Sankalia, *Studies in the Historical and Cultural Geography and Ethnography of Gujarat: 300 B.C.–1300 A.D.* (Poona: Deccan College P.G. & Research Institute, 1949), p. 9.
33. Ibid., p. 13.
34. James Bird, *History of Gujarat* (London: Richard Bentley, 1835).
35. H.G. Briggs, *The Cities of Gujarashtra* (Bombay: Times Press, 1849).
36. M.S. Commissariat, *A History of Gujarat* Vols. I and II (Bombay: Orient Longmans, 1958, 1957).
37. S.B. Rajyagore, *History of Gujarat* (New Delhi: S. Chand & Co., 1982).
38. Durgashankar Kevalram Shastri, *Gujaratno Madhyakalina Hindu Rajaputa Itihasa* (Ahmedabad: Gujarat Vidya Sabha, 1953).
39. Hari Prasad Shastri, *Gujaratno Prachina Itihasa* (Ahmedabad: Gujarat University, 1973).
40. Elaben Bhatt, *Gujarat ni Nari* (Gandhi Nagar: Government of Gujarat, 1974).
41. D.C. Sircar, *Indian Epigraphy* (Delhi: Motilal Banarasidas, 1965), p. 182.
42. K.V. Ramesh, *Indian Epigraphy* Vol. I (Delhi: Sandeep Prakashan, 1984), p. 29.
43. Ibid., p. 30.
44. Ibid.
45. Kumkum Roy, "Women and Men Donors at Sanchi: A Study of Inscriptional Evidence" in L.K. Tripathi (ed.), *Position and Status of Women in Ancient India* (BHU,1988).
46. Leslie Orr, "Women's Wealth and Worship: Female Patronage to Hinduism, Jainism and Buddhism in Medieval Tamilnadu" in Mandakranta Bose (ed.), *Faces of Feminine in Ancient Medieval and Modern India* (Delhi: OUP, 2000).

47. K.K. Shah, *The Problem of Identity: Women in Early Indian Inscriptions* (OUP, Delhi, 2001).
48. Ibid., p. 12.
49. *Gujarat Itihas Sandarbha Suchi*, Vols. I-VI (Ahmedabad: Gujarat Itihas Parishad, 1962–1972).
50. James Burgess & Bhagvanlal Indraji, *Inscriptions from the Cave Temples of Western India* (London: Indian Museum, 1881).
51. A.K. Forbes, *Rasmala,* Vol. I and II (London: OUP, 1924).
52. H.D. Sankalia, *Archaeology of Gujarat*, 1941.
53. H.D. Sankalia, *Studies in the Historical and Cultural Geography and Ethnography of Gujarat: 300 B.C.–1300 A.D.*, 1949.
54. H.G. Shastri, *A Historical and Cultural Study of the Inscriptions of Gujarat* (Ahmedabad: L.D. Institute, 1989).
55. Ramlal Parikh and Rasesh Jamindar, *Epigraphic Resources in Gujarat* (Delhi: Butala and Co., 1981).
56. PJLS, p. ii.
57. H.G. Shastri, op. cit., pp. 169–70.
58. Ibid., p. 170
59. R. Williams, *Jaina Yoga: Survey of Medieval Shravakacharas*, reprint, (Delhi: Motilal Banarasidas, 1999), p. xii.
60. Sagarmal Jain, "Jaina Dharma Men Nari Ki Bhoomika", in *Jaina Dharma Ki Pramukha Sadhviyam evam Mahilayem*, (Varanasi: P.V. Research Institute, 1991).
61. Hirabai Boradiya, op. cit.
62. K.K. Shah, op. cit., p. 17.
63. Clarence L. Barnhart and Robert K. Barnhart, *The World Book Dictionary*, Vol. II (Chicago: World Book inc., 1990), p. 1528.
64. Sylvia Walby, *Theorizing Patriarchy*, (Oxford, UK & Cambridge, USA: Blackwell, 1990), p. 19.
65. Ibid.
66. Ibid., p. 20.
67. Maithreyi Krishnaraj, *Contribution to Women's Studies*, Series-7 Feminist Concepts, Vol. I, p. 2. Bombay: RCWS, 1990.

# 2

# Women with Multiple Familial Attributes of Identity

## 11th Century C.E. to 14th Century C.E. (Period I)

This chapter contains the analysis of the inscriptions of period I (1000 C.E.–1400 C.E.). As a considerable number of the 13th century inscriptions are by the two ministers Vastupala and Tejapala, the inscriptions of this century have been sub-divided into V&T inscriptions (Vastupala and Tejapala) and non-V&T inscriptions.

This period is very important in the history of Gujarat, as well as in the history of Jainism. It is important for Gujarat because politically it became united and experienced prosperity as never before. It witnessed great activity in the fields of literature, art, architecture and sculpture during this period. That is why, the period from 10th century C.E. to 13th century C.E. is known as the golden period in the history of Gujarat.[1] Most of this period is also the most important period in the history of Jainism.[2] The period extending from 5th century C.E. to the end of 13th century C.E. saw the greatest achievements in Jaina literature, art and architecture. The two most important religions of Gujarat during this period were Hinduism and Jainism. Buddhism was extinct by this period, while Jainism attained more popularity.[3] The other two religions of the time were Islam and Zoroastrianism. Though the family religion of Caulukya kings was *Shaivism,* some of them also contributed to the construction and renovation of Jaina temples and patronised Jainism.[4] During Kumarapala's reign Jainism became the state religion. Their ministers also contributed to the cause of Jainism immensely. The most important among them were Vimala, who was appointed a *Dandanayaka* of Abu by Bhimadeva-I, and Vastupala and Tejapala, the ministers of Ranaka Virdhavala of Dholka.[5] The Caulukya rule ended at the beginning of the 14th century with the conquest of Gujarat by Ala-ud-din Khilji. Although there was great destruction of Jaina and Hindu temples during the initial plunder, the Jaina temple building activities continued in the 14th century C.E. Alpakhan, the Governor of Gujarat went to great lengths to ensure cordial relations with the Jaina merchants, as their continued prosperity was vital to his rule. Alpakhan not only allowed a wealthy merchant of Patan, Samarushah, to undertake the renovation of the temples of Shatrunjaya in 1315 C.E. but also made personal contribution to the project.[6] Pilgrimages were arranged to the Jaina *tirthas* like Shatrunjaya, Girnara and Abu. During these pilgrimages, people made their contributions to the temple building and renovating activities or donated images of *tirthankaras* and other gods and goddesses. The epigraphic records show that women not only took part in these activities but also recorded their contributions. Before analysing women's inscriptions, in order to have a comparative view, it is desirable to begin with considering men's inscriptions. A pattern of men's inscriptions has been drawn after going through men's inscriptions.

## Pattern of men's inscriptions

### *Non-V&T inscriptions*

In order to analyse the data from the gender perspective, as stated in the previous chapter, a few questions have been posed before the epigraphic records:

- Who were the persons forming the identity of the donor?

- For whose spiritual merit were the donations made or, in other words, who were the beneficiaries of the donations?
- What were the objects donated?

The sources have revealed the following pattern:

Men identify themselves with reference to their father's family. Some use only their father's name, some use the names of both the parents, while others use the lineage.

Many men donated for the spiritual merit of one of their close relatives. In this pattern father/mother/parents rank highest followed by, in descending order of preference, paternal uncle or brother, self, wife and son. Only a few donations were meant for the spiritual merit of sisters or daughters.

The above pattern fits perfectly with the patriarchal concept of family. Since sisters and daughters belonged to different families, donations meant for their spiritual benefit were very few.

Monks find mention in almost all the inscriptions as consecrators or motivators but nuns find mention very rarely.

Most of the men donated for objects like Jina images, *chaturvinshatipattas, siddhachakras* etc. Some men donated for *devakulikas* or small shrines. Donations involving large amounts such as building of a new temple or undertaking large-scale repairs came from a limited number of rich men. Up to the 13th century, this work was generally done by the ministers or, at times, by the kings. However, from the beginning of the 14th century, the responsibility was taken up by the rich merchants.

The donors of Pragvata and Shrimala communities appear most frequently in the records of this period. Some of the other castes finding mention in the records of this period are Ukesha, Modha, Gurjar etc.

This was the general pattern of men's records; however, a few records reflect variation from the above norm. Some such records are cited below:

1. Samvat 1202, Ashadha sudi 6, Monday; an image of Shantinatha, dedicated by Maham. Valana and Dhavala for

the merit of Shantimati, their mother; Shantimati being the wife of Dhanadeva, son of Asadeva of Pragvata caste and daughter (*sutaa*) of Volha and Shilai, --- (*PJLS-II*,139, Abu)

2. Samvat 1249, Jyeshtha shudi 10, Monday; Neminatha, dedicated for the merit of his wife Ratni by Chahada; Ratni being the daughter (*sutaa*) of Shre. Dadu --- (*PLS-I*, 25, Wadhvan)
3. Samvat 1334, Radha sudi 10, Sunday; a *parikara* and an image of Suvidhinatha, dedicated for the merit of his sister (*bhagini*) Suhada by Lunasingha, son of ... of Shri Shrimali caste --- (*PJLS-II*,498, Abu)
4. Samvat 1378; dedicated for the merit of daughter (*putri*) Nau by Narada, Madana, Puna, Padama and Salakha, sons of Sa. Savada. (*PJLS-II*, 196, Abu)
5. Samvat 1379; an image of Shri Mahaviradeva, --- dedicated for the merit of sister (*bhagini*) Dharani *sushravika* by Sha. Dhadala, Sha. Gayadhara, Sha. Dhirachandra, the *sushravakas*, along with their family; the donors being the sons of Sha. Sahajapala --- (*Shat*, 118, Shatrunjaya)

In (1) above Mahan, Valana and Dhavala have donated for the spiritual merit of their mother. The donors, instead of giving their identity directly, do so indirectly by giving their mother's identity. She has been identified as wife of Dhanadeva, as well as daughter of Volha and Shilai. Thus, the donors mention their paternal as well as maternal family. This is a clear variation from the norms of identification prevailing.

Inscriptions (3) and (5) are the donations whose beneficiaries are the sisters of the donors. In (3) Lunasiha donates for the spiritual merit of his sister Suhada and in (5) three brothers along with their family have donated for the spiritual merit of their sister Dharani. In (4) the donation is meant for the daughter. This record is very brief. The donors are brothers who are donating for the spiritual merit of Nau, who seems to be the daughter of one of them. (2) again is a case where the norms of identification have not been followed. Donor Chahada gives only his personal name, but identifies his wife Ratni, for whose merit the donation is meant, as Dadu's daughter. Here, it seems, the donor thought it more appropriate to associate himself with Dadu, his father-in-law. In this record the donor's self-perception can be clearly seen.

The above examples together represent variations from the norms, which reflected patriarchal values in most of the available records.

### *V&T inscriptions*

In this collection, there are forty-seven inscriptions of Vastupala and Tejapala, belonging to the period V.S. (Vikrama Samvat) 1278–1297. They differ from the other inscriptions in the following matters.

They donate for the spiritual merit of all their relatives, wives, daughters, daughters-in-law, sons, sisters and so on. However, they do not donate for the merit of their parents. It could be because their father had married a widow (their mother) and so Vastupala and Tejapala did not want to bring their parents in bold relief.

In some of their records, wives find respectable mention and are eulogised. The lineage of the wife's paternal family is also given. However, women of their family never appear as donors in their inscriptions.

Vastupala and Tejapala were brothers and came from a Jaina family belonging to Pragvata (Porvad) community. They were ministers of King Viradhavala of Dholka, who was a feudatory king of Bhima-II of Anhilawad Patana. Both the brothers were not only shrewd politicians and successful generals but also great patrons of learning, men of religious devotion and great builders of monuments such as the temples on Mt. Abu and Girnar.[7] The temple of Neminatha, erected by Tejapala on Mt. Abu in V.S. 1287, is an outstanding one, and the best ever erected by a minister of Gujarat.[8] This temple was meant for the spiritual merit of his first wife Anupamadevi and Lavanyasimha, their son, according to the inscription in this temple.[9] This inscription gives the lineage of Anupama's father. It eulogises her parents and praises Anupama. It has been said about her that, with her virtues she has illuminated both the families, the family of her father and that of her in-laws. Tejapala spent crores of rupees towards constructing this temple for his first wife Anupama, but he also did spend some lacs for his second wife Suhadadevi.[10]

Vastupala, the elder brother of Tejapala, also constructed temples on Girnar for himself and his two wives.[11] He has also constructed some other temples on Shatrunjaya.[12]

There are no records in the present collection, in which wives of Vastupala and Tejapala figure as donors, though they also probably came from rich families. From the textual sources[13] it seems that Tejapala's wife Anupamadevi, was a very intelligent person, who took keen interest in literature and philosophy. She has been credited with the composition of *Kankanakavya.* Vastupala and Tejapala respected her advice in all matters. She constantly supervised the building of the Abu temple and it was at her instance that the artisans working there were provided with amenities like food and rest.

Patriarchy was the ideology of those times. It is only recently that the justification of patriarchy is being questioned. It is true that under the patriarchal system the male members of the family are placed in a favourable position. However, they are also expected to take care of all the needs of their dependents. From epigraphic evidence, it seems that Vastupala and Tejapala, as responsible male members of the family, took care of all the needs of their family members, including their religious need of gaining spiritual merit. The needs of their wives were also well taken care of. Though Anupama does not figure as the donor, she is well represented in V&T inscriptions. The very fact that Tejapala spent crores of rupees for her speaks volumes about her influence on him.

A lot about Anupama is known from the textual sources but we have no way to know about her perception. Not even a single epigraph is available. It is quite possible that respecting the values of her times, she let her husband do everything, herself taking a secondary position.

After having made certain observations about the men's records from the inscriptional sources, it is time now to analyse women's inscriptions.

## Women's inscriptions

For this period, there are a little less than hundred inscriptions in which women figure as donors. This is approximately 9 per cent of the total inscriptions that belong to this period.

Women's records have been studied under six heads:

1. Women with wifely,attribute of identity.
2. Women with daughterly attribute of identity.
3. Women with two or more familial attributes.
4. Women using only personal name as the attribute of identity.
5. The solitary daughter-in-law.
6. Women renouncers.

Just like the men's inscriptions, women's inscriptions also follow the set pattern. According to this pattern, first day, date and year of donation is given followed by the caste and/or religious affiliation of the donor. Then comes the name of the donor and her familial and other attributes of identity. Next, the object donated and the name of the monk who consecrated the image are mentioned Sometimes, the place of origin of the donor is given in the beginning or in the end. Throughout the centuries, this pattern was followed. However, some of the donors make variations in their record, which provide us with valuable information.

## Women with wifely attribute of identity

Below are cited a few representative inscriptions in this category. In this collection, some are stereotypical records and some are those in which minor variations have been made.

1. Samvat 1112, Phaguna vadi 1, Monday; an image of Parshvanatha, dedicated for the merit of Shre. Nagara by his wife *(bharya)* Tihunadevi, --- *(JDLS-II*, Khambat)
2. Samvat 1182; --- dedicated for the merit of self by Lahita, wife *(bharya)* of Parama (brahma) and her daughter

(*putrika*) Sita. Parma (brahma) being the son of Varunaga. (*RPLS, 12,* Radhanpur)

3. Samvat 1212, Magha sudi 10; dedicated for the merit of self by Jasuka, wife (*bharya*) of Maham. Shri Jajjaka at Abu, --- (*PJLS-II, 221*, Abu)
4. 90, Samvat 1226, Jyeshtha sudi 8, Thursday; an image of Parshvanatha, dedicated by Ruvini along with Lakhman, Palhana, Delhana; Ruvini being the wife (*patni*) of Apingana, --- (*Nir*, p. 346)
5. Samvat 1302, Chaitra vadi 11, Monday; dedicated by *shravika* (name lost), wife (*bharya*) of Kuara of Pragvata caste, inhabitant of Chandravati, ... (*PJLS-II*, 115, Abu)
6. Samvat 1305, Jyeshtha shudi 11, Mondy; an image of Rohini, dedicated by Tha. Salshana devi, wife (*bharya*) of Tha. Sanga of Pragvata caste. (*PLS-I*, 41, Dabhoda)
7. Samvat 1331, Vaishakha vadi 7; Shri *chaturvinshatipatta*, dedicated for the merit of self by Jayatu vyavaharika, along with son Vya.Bhacha and family, Jayatu being the wife (*bharya*) of Tha. Jayatasingh of Shadayatha caste. (*JDLS-II*, 147, Vadodara)
8. Samvat 1378; an image of Mallinatha, dedicated for the merit of self by Bakai *shravika*, wife (*bharya*) of Lakhmana, son of Sa. Vika. (*PJLS-II*, 189, Abu)
9. ... a *samavasarana* dedicated by Dilhanadevi and Dhandaladevi, wives (*bharya*) of Vijada --- (*PJLS-II*, 167, Abu)
10. Samvata 139, Vaishakha sudi 3; an image of Shri Neminatha, dedicated for the merit of self by Vya. Ratnadivya, wife (*bharya*) of Vya. Munjala, son of Vya. Deva, descendent of Shre. Paja of Modha race --- (*PLS-I*, 67, Wadhvan)
11. Samvat 1408; a *panchatirthi* image of Adinatha, dedicated for the merit of Maham. Dharaniga, his beloved (*priya*) Muhagade and their son Jasada of Pragvata caste by Sarini, daughter-in-law (*vadhu*) of Dharaniga and Muhagade and wife (*vadhu*) of Jasada (*JDLS-II*, 141, Vadodara)

12. Samvat 1442, Vaishakha vadi 10, Sunday; an image of *Jivitasvami* Shri Adinatha, dedicated for the merit of self by Hiradevi, wife (*bharya*) of Shre. Harapala of Shri Shrimali caste --- (*JPLS*, 161, Tharad)

In all the inscriptions cited above, the donor women express their identity in terms of their wifely status. They give the names of their husbands and their personal names. The name of the husband invariably comes first, indicating the importance attached to it. In many cases, the husband's name is preceded by his father's/parent's name and his caste. Usually the word *bharya* is used to indicate the wifely status. A few women donors prefer the word *patni* to indicate their wifely status.

The citations (3) (5) (6) (8) and (10) are stereotypical records. However, even in these records the donors have made slight variations. The donor of (5), whose personal name is lost, has chosen to use the religious attribute of *shravika* in addition to her wifcly attribute. Similarly, Bakai, the donor of (8), has also used the attribute *shravika*. In both the cases, their religious attribute has come after their wifely attribute. This suggests that in the opinion of these donors their wifely attribute was more important than their religious attribute. The donors of citations (6) and (10) have used the professional attributes in addition to their wifely attributes. In both cases, the professional attributes of the husband and wife are the same. Salasanadevi of (6) takes the professional attribute *thakur* or *thakurain*.[14] Ratnadivya of (10) has used the feminine form of *vyavahari*.

Tihunadevi of (1) and Sarini of (11) have donated for the religious merit of their respective husbands. Tihunadevi donates solely for her husband and Sarini donates for the benefit of her husband and her in-laws. She calls herself their *vadhu*. She has used this word probably because it associates her with her in-laws and her husband at the same time.

Inscriptions (2), (4) and (7) are group donation in which women are the chief donors. In (2) Lahita and her daughter Sita are the donors. The word *putrika* has been used to indicate Sita's daughterly status. *Putrika* is a term, which differentiates between the ordinary daughter and the one whose son is the heir to her parent's property.[15]

Thus, in a way, it is similar to (4) and (7) where women have associated their sons in their donations. Jayatu of (7), apart from her wifely attribute, has also used the professional attribute (*vyavaharika*). In those days it was fairly common for women to take feminine forms of the professional attributes. What distinguishes Jayatu from other women is that her professional attribute is different from that of her husband. Her husband's attribute is tha, meaning *thakkura*. Jayatu's attribute is vayava, i.e. vyavahari or a merchant. Her son's attribute is also *vyavahari*. Jayatu's taking the professional attribute not of her husband, but that of her son could be seen in the light of several reasons. The most likely possibility is that she was the daughter of a merchant and so took the title. Another possibility is that her husband was dead, and so she took the professional attribute of her son. However, as she is the chief donor she must not have been financially dependent on him. According to the Jaina law, wife was first the heir of a man, not the son. The third possibility is that she herself was a merchant in her own right. Considering the social norm of the period, this seems less likely; nevertheless, it cannot be ruled out altogether. Another thing worth noting about this record is the similarity between the names of Jayatu and her husband Jayatasingh. There are many more records in which the names of husband and wife are similar. It seems that there was a practice of changing the wife's name to suit that of her husband. Jayatu followed the social norm while identifying herself. She used the wifely attribute of identity. Her personal name had also been changed to suit that of her husband. However, she has also retained her own identity, independent of her husband's, by adopting her own professional attribute.

In (9) two women, who are co-wives have come together to donate. In the patriarchal society of Gujarat, polygamy was prevalent. It was expected of the co-wives that they stay together harmoniously. The two women seem to fulfil this ideal laid down by the society.[16]

Hiradevi of (12) has donated the image of Shri Adinatha. She has used the term *jivitasvami* in her record. There are a few records where men have used this term. However, the women used the term more often. This record, which belongs to the second half of 14th century, is the only record of the period in which the term *jivitasvami* has been used. All other records in which this term has been used belong to period II. Lodha[17] is of the opinion that the *saubhagyavati* women, i.e., the women whose husbands were alive, mostly used the term. Men used it to indicate that at the time of donation, their parents were alive. Lodha also adds that if a donor does not use the term, it does not mean that his/her parents/husband were dead. This explanation seems quite plausible. The term also indicates that the image represents a lifetime portrait of the *tirthankara*. In his book, U.P. Shah states that probably attempts were made to worship an image of Mahavira during his lifetime. A portrait statue of sandalwood was supposed to have been made when Mahavira was standing in meditation in his own palace, about a year or two before his final renunciation. Therefore, the statue showed a crown, some ornaments and a lower garment on the person of Mahavira. Being a lifetime portrait statue it was known as *jivitasvami or jivantasvami pratima*, that is, image fashioned during the lifetime of the Lord. All later images of this iconographic type then came to be known as *jivitasvami or jivantasvami pratimas*. This concept remained popular in the medieval period and was later applied to images of other *tirthankaras*.[18] Whether the mention of *jivitasvami* in the records mentioned above is made in order to indicate the iconographic type or the marital status of the women donating that image can be ascertained to some extent only after looking at the images on which the term appears.

### Women with daughterly attribute of identity

Below are cited a few records where women have used their daughterly status:

1. 9 Samvat 1157, Vaishakha sudi 10; --- an image of Shri Suparshvanathadeva, dedicated for the merit of her daughter Suhava by Tha. Rajuka, daughter (*sutaa*) of Tha. Subhadra of Ranteja. (*PJLS-II*, 466, Ranteja)
2. Samvat 1168, Vaishakha sudi 10; an image of Shri Mahavira, dedicated for the merit of self by Papai, daughter (*putrika*) of Vardhamana of Savadevacharya *gaccha* (*JDLS-II*, 1083, Khambat)
3. Samvat 1207, Chaitra vadi 5, Saturday; --- two images of Shri Ajitanathajin dedicated for the merit of self by Strami and Sanpi, daughters (*duhita*) of Shre. Shanti. (*PLS-I*, 10, Wadhvan)
4. Samvat 1218, Chaitra vadi 5, Saturday; an image of Shri Shantijina, dedicated for the merit of self by Sahaji, daughter (*putrika*) of Jasadhavala. --- (*Nir.* p. 345, No. 5)
5. Samvat 1293, Chaitra vadi 8, Friday; an image of Shri Parshvanatha in this small shrine (*devakulika*) situated in Shri. Neminatha deva temple (*chaitya*) situated in the Lunasinghavasahika, dedicated for the merit of her mother by Ratnadevi, daughter (*sutaa*) of Maham. Shri. Sobhanadeva and his wife Maham. Shri. Mau—of Pragvata caste. (*PJLS-II*, 101, Abu)
6. Samvat 1302, Margashirsha vadi 9, Saturday; an image of Shrimadadinatha along with the *parikara*, dedicated for the merit of self by Thehika, daughter (*putri*) of Maham. Chahada, son of Man. Palla, at the advice of Shri Devabhadrasuri --- (*PJLS-II*, 210, Abu)
7. Samvat 1303, Pra. Magha sudi 14, Monday; an image of Shantinathadeva, dedicated for the merit of self by Somi, daughter (*putrika*) of Sa. Chandra, son of Sa. Punda of Pallivala caste. (*Shat*, 103, Shatrunjaya)
8. Samvat 1394; an image of Shri Adinatha, dedicated for the merit of self by Manishi, daughter (*putri*) of Sa.Vijapala--- (*APJLS*, 77, Abu)

9. Samvat 1394; an image of Adinatha, dedicated for the merit of self by Bo, daughter (*putri*) of Dhanapala --- (*PJLS-II*, 178)
10. Samvat 1394; an image of Shitalanatha, dedicated for the merit of self by Chachuladevi, daughter (*putri*) of San. Dhadha, son of San. Udayaraja --- (*PJLS-II*, 228, Abu)

Women appearing in these inscriptions use only their daughterly status as a mark of their identity, without even mentioning the names of their husbands. The terms used to indicate daughterly status are *duhita, sutaa, putri* and *putrika.*

Under the then prevailing social structure it was expected that they at least name their husbands. Since they have not done so it logically follows that they were either unmarried or child-widows. However, the donor of inscription (1) was certainly not so, because she is donating for the spiritual merit of her daughter. This inscription is in fact a clear case of self-perception. Raghuka, the daughter of Subhadra, has donated the image of Parshvanatha for the religions merit of her daughter Suhava. Thus, Raghuka, in spite of being married, chooses to use her daughterly status, that too with reference to her mother alone. Further, Raghuka also takes the professional attribute tha. meaning *thakkura* (or the feminine form of it). *Thakkura* means a village chief or a petty landholder. They were expected to wield arms in defence of their property. A *thakkura* is supposed to be *a Kshatriya Or Rajput.* However, this was not true in all cases. In Caulukya period, and perhaps even later, *Thakkura* was also associated with *Brahmans, Kayasthas* etc. The title was used with reference to persons who appear to be merchants, writers and even women; it appears that thakkura was a title applied irrespective of the caste of the person bearing it. This title might have been denoting a small feudal chief or a *Jagirdara.*[19]

The donor of inscription (2), Papai, Sahaji of (4) and Somi of (7) were also in all probability, married women. The reason for drawing this inference is that they use the term *putrika* to express their daughterly status. The term *putrika* has a legal aspect. This term indicates that they were the daughters of sonless fathers on whom son-hood was ascribed.[20] A *putrika* was expected to raise male issue for her father.[21] In ancient times, according to Hindu Law, when a man had no son he could make his daughter do for a son i.e. make her *putrika,* and stipulate with the person marrying her that the son born of her would be his (i.e. the girl's father's) son and would offer *pindas* as a son to his maternal grandfather.[22] No doubt the term is used in Hindu law, but in the Jaina law also we find a provision where a sonless man could make his daughter and her son the heir to his property.[23] However, whether the term *putrika* was used in the Jaina law or not, could not be ascertained. Nevertheless, that the term was in vogue among the Jainas of Gujarat is clear from the epigraphic evidence. As this word appears in a few Jaina inscriptions, there is reason to believe that Jainas of this period must be practicing the concept of *putrika*. For Jainas a son was not required to offer *pindas* to his father, but to carry on the family lineage and as an heir to the property, a son was no doubt needed. As Sahaji, Somi and Papai were probably legal heirs to their fathers it was obvious for them to use their daughterly status. They could have easily mentioned their husbands' names nevertheless but the fact that they did not do so indicates that self-perception rather than social construction of identity was more important for them.

The donor women of (3), (6), (8), (9) and (10) have identified themselves with reference to their fathers alone, whereas Ratanadevi of (5) identifies herself with reference to both her parents. She has donated for the religions merit of her mother. Apart from her familial attribute of identity, which of course comes first, she has also used the professional attribute, thakkura to identify herself. Her professional attribute (or the feminine form of it) is different from that of her parents. This could probably mean that she was married to a thakkura. In the previous section we noted that there was one woman Jayatu, who identified herself with reference to her husband but used the professional attribute different from that of her husband. Here is a woman who has identified herself with reference to her parents, but has taken a professional title different from that of her parents. She has not indicated her marital status. These two examples indicate that some women exercised their choice while using the attributes of their identity.

K.K. Shah, in his book, states that "The commonest way to constitute social identity for a Jaina woman was to mention her four fold familial status of a daughter, a daughter-in-law, a wife and a mother, and normally given in the same chronological order".[24] However, while going through the Jaina inscriptions of Gujarat belonging to 2nd millennium C.E., it becomes clear that there are hardly any inscriptions where women have mentioned their fourfold familial status. Regional dimension and a gap of at least a thousand years could explain the change. However, there are a few cases where women have used two or three familial attributes of identity.

## Women with two or more familial attributes of identity

Below are offered a few citations where women have used two or more attributes of identity:

1. Samvat 1270 ... ; an image of Shri Parshvanatha, dedicated for the merit of Dhanasingh, son of Shre. Umbha by his mother (*matru*), Ja .... Consecrated by --- (*RPLS*, 26, Radhanpura).
2. Samvat 1300, Jyeshtha shudi 5, Thursday; ... for the merit of self by Maham. Vayajaladevi, (along with?) son Tha. Rajasinghvaradeva; Vayajaladevi being the wife (*bharya*) of Maham. Ranasingh, son of Maham. Vairasingh, ... and daughter of Tha. Jagasaha --- (*JDLS-I*, 514, Visanagara)
3. Samvat 1303; an image of Shri Neminatha along with the small shrine (*khattaka*) in the temple (*chaitya*) of Shri. Adinatha, dedicated for the merit of self by Virika, wife/beloved (*pranayini*) of Tha. Shridhara, son of Tha. Udyapala of Kantala caste; the donor also being the daughter (*putri*) of Tha. Naga, and mother (*janani*) of Ambadevasingh --- (*PJLS-II*, 209, Abu)
4. Samvat 1378; Mahavira (an image of) dedicated for the merit of self by Nivini *shravika*, daughter (*putri*) of Sharnivala Petha and his wife Palhanadevi, and (sister) of

their son Luna; Nivini also being the wife of Sangha. Sadhala Pushagana --- (*PJLS-II*, 183, Abu)

In inscription (1) the donor's proper name is lost. She has given her husband's name and her son's name. However, her husband's name comes not as the attribute of her identity but as that of her son's identity. Similarly, her son's name comes not as her identity but as a person for whose benefit the donation has been made. Her personal name, though coming in the end, is the most important attribute of her identity.

The donor of the inscription (2), Vayjaladevi, has constituted her identity with reference to her husband and her father. Some portion of this record is lost, but it seems that it is a group inscription, Vayjaladevi is the chief donor, and her sons Rajsingh, Varadeva are the associated donors. Another possibility is that she is giving the name of her sons to indicate her motherly status.

In any case, it seems her wifely attribute is the most important attribute in her opinion. This is because firstly it comes first among her familial attributes and secondly because she takes the title of mahanta, which is the same as that of her husband.

Inscription(3) above is one of the rare inscriptions where a woman has used her threefold identity. She first states her wifely attribute using the term *pranayini*. This word means a mistress, a beloved wife or a female friend.[25] In the corpus of inscriptions collected for the present study, there are only a couple of records making use of the term *pranayini*. In a polygamous society it is quite possible that either Virika, the donor of this record, was not a legally wedded wife of Shridahara or that she was a wedded wife, but in her opinion, the most loved one. Another record making use of the term is that of Soni Tejapala (*Shat* 10). Here it has been used in the meaning of wife, probably the first or the only wife. The record belongs to the sixteenth century. In Virika's record too, it appears that the term has been used for indicating her wifely status. Besides, as Virika has also given the name of her father, she could not have been a mistress. It could be that the choice of word *pranayini* is made to stress the fact that she was more close to her husband than his other wives were. Next in the chronology of attributes is her daughterly attribute with reference to her father alone, and the last comes her motherly attribute.

In the inscription (4), the donor Nivini uses three attributes of identity. First, she gives her daughterly status with reference to her father as well as mother. In fact, she goes a step further and names her brother. Probably she has tried to indicate her place as a daughter in her father's family. Next comes her religions attribute *shravika*, and in the end comes her husband's name.

Thus, it can be seen that in the inscription (2) the donor Vayjaladevi, has used a set-pattern to record her donation. The donors of other three records have made some variations in their records and have shown a grater degree of autonomy in constituting their identity. Virika has chosen the term *pranayini* to indicate her wifely status, highlighting the importance attached to this relationship by her. Niviai was proud of her daughterly status and had a sense of belonging to her natal family, whereas, the donor of inscription (1) was a person of independent identity.

## Women with personal names only

Some women have used only personal names to identify themselves. Below are given a few such records:

1. Samvat 1259; dedicated for the merit of her daughter (*duhitru*) Somati by Suhana *shravika*. (*RPLS*, 9, Radhanpur)
2. Samvat 1226, Ashadha sudi 9, Thursday; an image of Viranatha, dedicated for the merit by Pahavada Murika ... *shrethani shravika* --- (*Shat*, 455, Shatrunjaya)
3. Samvat 1234, Margashirsha sudi 15, Friday; --- an image of Shri Mahavira dedicated for the merit of self by Ǵunadevi, — (Nir, No. 7, p. 346)
4. Samvat 1361, Phalguna shudi 3, Thursday; --- an image of Ambika *devi* dedicated for the merit of self by Bai Suhaba, disciple of *sadhvi* Malayasundari --- (*PJLS-II*, 522, Patan)
5. Samvat 1378; --- (dedicated by) Va.Vayajalade, Va. Pulaka, Va. Lavama of Pragvata caste --- (*Shat*, 356, Shatrunjaya)

The women donors appearing in these records have not used any familial attribute of identity. However, some of them have used other non-familial attributes of identity. Suhana, of the first inscription, calls herself *shravika*. She has donated for the religious merit of her daughter somati. Murika of (2) uses *shretani* and *shravika* as her attributes of identity.[26] Perhaps her husband was a *shresthi*. Her taking the feminine form of this title indicates that she took pride in being a *shretani*. Her religious attribute *shravika* comes next in the chronology of attributes. Inscription (4) is a unique record in two ways. Firstly, because it is one of the few records in which nuns find mention. In this record, a nun (*sadhvi*) is not only just mentioned but is respectfully mentioned as the teacher of the donor. Secondly, it shows a greater degree of self-perception on the part of the donor. She has associated herself with her teacher *sadhvi* Malayasundari. Bai Suhaba, the donor of this record, has called herself the disciple of *sadhvi* Malayasundari. She did not feel it necessary to give any other attribute of her identity. She seems to be of a spiritual bent of mind. It is quite possible that she was thinking of opting out of the family and becoming a nun. Gunadevi of (3) has given just her personal name, while the donors of (5) have given their caste in addition to their personal names.

### The solitary daughter-in-law

1. Samvat 1382, Vaishakha vadi 8, Friday; an image of Parshvanatha, dedicated for the merit of her husband Chacha by Chahinidevi, daughter-in-law (*vadhu*) of Vya. Dhanapala and his wife Dhadaladevi of Pragvata caste --- (*APJLS*, 552)

This is one of the very few epigraphic records where a woman has used her daughter-in-law status by using the term *vadhu*. There is one more record where a woman, Sarini has used the term *vadhu*. However, there she uses it with reference to her in-laws as well as husband.[27]

No doubt, many women who used their wifely attribute to identify themselves mentioned the names of their in-laws. However, that formed the part of the husband's identity. In this particular record, the donor Cahini has used the names of her in-laws to identify herself, though she donated for the spiritual merit of her husband. This indicates the importance attached to this relationship by Cahini.

Jainism allowed women to renounce the world and become nuns. The four-fold Jaina community consists of *sadhus, sadhvis, shravakas and shravikas*. In these epigraphic records, *sadhus, shravakas* and *shravikas* are well represented, but the mention of *sadhvis* is very rare. For period I there are a few records in which *sadhvis* find mention. Below are cited all these inscriptions.

**Women renouncers**

1. Om. This is the religious gift of *ganini* Acchupta of Shri Vijayatungacharya *gaccha* Shaka Samvat 930 (C.E. 1008). The image has been fashioned by Govinda. (*Nir*, p. 67 Bharucha)
2. Samvat 1360, Ashadha vadi 4; Shri. Divakaracharya, disciple of Shri Jinaprabodhasuri, disciple of Jineshwarsuri of Khartar *gaccha*, Pan. Laxminivasagani, Hematilakagani, Matikalashamuni, Munichandramuni, Amararatnagani, Yashakiritmuni, along with the fourfold *sangha* of monks, nuns and others, daily offer their satutations (*pranamanti*) to Shri Adinatha, Shri Neminatha, --- (*APJLS*, 317, Abu)
3. Samvat 1361, Phalguna shudi 3, Thursday; — an image of Ambika *devi* dedicated for the merit of self by Bai Suhaba, disciple of *sadhvi* Malayasundari --- (*PJLS-II*, 522,. Patan) (Same as (4) of women with personal name alone)
4. Samvat 1421, Jyeshtha sudi 10,Wednesday ---; a small shrine (*devakulika*) in the temple (*chaitya*) of Shri Parshvanatha, dedicated for the merit of self by *sadhvi* Bhavaladevi, along with --- descendants of Visata, of Upakesha caste and Chichata *gotra* --- (*JPLS*, 303-A, Jiraula)
5. --- Samvat 1430, Mahasudi 15; a *chaturvinshatiptta* dedicated by Soni Prathamasingh and his wife (*bharya*) Shrimalade, their son Soni Singha and his wife (*bharya*) Shri

Ghangha, their son Januka and his wife (*patni*) Kosalade; with the advice of *bhattraka* Shri Jayanandasuri Shri. Devasundarasuri—*mahattaraa* Charitrashri; --- (*Shat*, 76, Shatrunjaya)

In all the five records nuns find mention in different capacities. In (1) above a nun finds mention as a donor. Nun as a donor! Sounds contradictory. When the renouncers were not supposed to own or posses any thing, how could they donate? One explanation could be that while entering the order she must have donated her possessions. However, in this citation, it seems that Accupta had been a nun for some time as she has taken the title *ganini,* which indicates that she was the head of a group.[28] *Sadhvi* Bhavaladevi, of citation (4) also figures as the donor. Though the phraseology of this record is not very clear but one thing is certain that it is a record of a group donation by the descendants of Visata of Upakesha caste and Chivata *gotra* and *sadhvi* Bhavaladevi is the chief donor. In the record, the name Bhavaladevi appears twice, once as Mahana's (one member of the group) wife and second time as the chief donor *sadhvi* Bhavaldevi. It could be that Mahana's wife Bhavaladevi had become a nun and in order to give her due respect, she has been made the chief donor, though expenses might have been borne by other male members of the group. The record indicates that the women who became nuns were greatly respected by their family members. There are also a few cases in which monks were the donors.[29] Nevertheless, such cases were rare. The observation of Dr K.K. Shah,[30] that the Jaina renounces rarely figure as donors, holds good for the period and province of this study also.

In inscription (3), a nun figures as the teacher or preceptor of a woman. *Bai* Suhaba, it seem, takes pride in calling herself the disciple of *sadhvi* Malayasundari. *Mahattaraa* Shricaritrashri, of (5) finds mention alongside two other monks as the motivator of a family of donors. The title *mahattaraa* of the nun suggests that she was an old and respected member of the group.[31] In this record her name comes after the names of two other monks. The wording of the inscription is not clear. The names of two monks before the name of the nun could mean either that they were her preceptors and seniors or that they along with the nun were the motivators of the family mentioned in the record. If the second possibility is true, then it corroborates the literary prescription that the nuns, however senior, and learned, were inferior to monks.[32] In citation (2) no particular nun finds mention. Names of a few monks are mentioned and the nuns are mentioned collectively by using the term *sadhvi* as part of *sadhusadhvichaturvidha-sangha.*

The paucity of records mentioning nuns and the phraseology of the records, both indicate the secondary status of *sadhvis* vis-à-vis *sadhus*. However, the records also show that in spite of these limitations, some nuns, by the dint of their merit became preceptors and motivators. They rose to the position where they commanded the respect of the people.

**Sculpted images of nuns:** The depiction of *acharyas* in stone and to a lesser extent in painting, is deeply rooted in Jaina tradition.[33] but the images of nuns are a rarity.

Three sculpted images of nuns were brought to light by *muni* Shri Yashovijayaji.[34] The earliest of these three images belongs to the 12th century (V.S. 1205). It is a standing image of a nun. On both sides of the image, two *upasikas* or *shravikas* have been shown. The inscription on this image reads—*Samvat 1205 Shri mahattaraa sa parivara*. The image is in the personal collection of *muni* Yashovijayaji. The second image shows a nun seated surrounded by *shravikas*. This is in a temple at Patan. The inscription on the image—*V.S. 1255, Kartika vadi 11, Dematiganini murty*. The third image is dated 1298 V.S. It is from Matar *tirtha* near Kheda. A nun is shown in a sitting posture, showing reverence to a Jina image kept on her head. However, for years the people took this image to be that of Gautama Svani, the disciple of Lord Mahavira, holding the image of Mahavira on his head. Yashovijayaji removed this misconception of the people sometime before 1956 C.E. The inscription below the image gives the name of the nun as Aryapadamasiri.

The fact that the people of the 20th century could not even imagine that the image of a nun could exist, shows their androcentric bias. Against this background, the fact that at least a few images of nuns were sculpted and perhaps worshipped in the 13th century is quite important. There is no information as to when the practice of worshipping the images of monks was introduced. Therefore, it is very difficult to say whether the practice of worshipping monks' images preceded that of worshipping nuns' images or not. It is quite possible that the practice of worshipping monks' and nuns' images was introduced at the same time, but nuns' images were less frequent than monks' images. This is quite natural for a period when male superiority was taken for granted. The earliest literary reference to the images of nuns is found in a 15th century work *Acharadinakara.* The author of this book has given the ritual of consecration of the *sadhvi* images.[35]

*Muni* Yashovijayji is of the opinion that the custom of worshipping nuns' images could have been introduced to bring parity between monks and nuns, at least, as far as showing veneration to them is concerned. However, what is more probable is that the custom was introduced for inculcating the value of renunciation in the minds of women lay followers. It can be seen that in two of the three sculptures mentioned above, *shravikas* have also been depicted. Besides, in the past, religion was the driving force behind all art, architecture and literature. The Jaina thinkers discussed the question of gender only when women's ability to attain *moksha* was debated. Though the Shvetambara Jainas acknowledged that women could attain *moksha,* they never thought of women as equal to men.

## Pattern of women's inscriptions

As far as the pattern of identification is concerned, there does not seem to be a single pattern. A variety of familial attributes was available to them. Women exercised their choice and used those attributes of identity, which suited them the most.

Some women opted for their wifely attribute while others chose their daughterly attribute. However not all women who opted for a daughterly attribute were necessarily unmarried. A few women used two or more familial attributes, while others did not use any familial attribute at all. These women either identified themselves by using only personal names or used religious, professional or some other attribute along with their personal name. Thus, the identification pattern of women suggests that women enjoyed some autonomy in the epigraphic space offered to them.

Most of the women donated for the spiritual merit of their own selves. Some have not mentioned the beneficiary of their donation at all. Only in a few cases were the donations meant for the spiritual merit of one of the close relatives. There is one example of a donation for the spiritual merit of mother, one for parents and one for son. In two cases the beneficiaries were daughters whereas four women donated for the spiritual merit of their husbands. All of these four women belonged to the 14th century. Thus, it seems that while selecting the beneficiaries of donations, most of the women of period I followed the set pattern.

Objects donated by women were the same as those donated by men. Almost all women have donated for objects like *chaturvinshatipattas, Jina images* and the like. Just two or three women have donated for the objects involving middle level investment like construction of *devakulikas.* There is no epigraphic record of any donation involving large sums by women of this period. However, the literary sources mention two women who donated for the construction of temples. Nittaladevi built a temple of Parshvanatha at Patadi and some time before 1136 C.E. Hansi *bai* added a *mandapa* to the extant Neminatha temple at Kunbharia.[36]

Most of the women donors of this period came from the two castes Srimala and Pragvata. One each came for Ukesha and Vayada, whereas two women donors belonged to Gurjara caste.

## Comparison between patterns of men's and women's inscriptions

As has been indicated earlier, the question of men's identity was a simple one (much like today) as they were not required to change their families after marriage. Almost all men identified themselves with reference to their father's families. They used either the father's name or parents' name or the lineage. The other attributes of their identity were caste, profession, religious affiliation or/and place of origin. Therefore, it can be said that as far as the self-identification pattern is concerned most of the men were largely governed by patriarchy.

Patriarchy indicates a system of male dominance. In India too, the lawgivers, Hindu as well as Jaina, expected women to always remain under the control of male members of their families. Unmarried girls were to stay under the control and protection of their fathers, married women under the control and protection of their husbands, and for widows the sons were the protectors. Women were indoctrinated into the system and therefore they identified themselves with reference to their fathers, husbands, sons etc. Therefore, all those cases where women identified themselves with reference to their husbands could be indicative of the hold of patriarchy on these women. Similarly, all these cases where unmarried women or girls identified themselves as daughters, especially with reference to their fathers, also indicates the hold of patriarchy on these women or girls. However, how should we interpret the cases where women, though married, identified themselves, with reference to their father alone? In my opinion, such cases are also indicative of the patriarchal values. These women, no doubt, exercised their choice of selecting the daughterly attribute as the mark of their identity, but they also saw themselves under the protection of their fathers. Among the women using their daughterly attribute of identity, very few have identified themselves with reference to both the parents. There is only one case where a woman has identified herself with reference to her mother alone. In a little more than 20 per cent of the women's records women did not use any familial attribute at all. About such women it could perhaps be said that they were not greatly governed by patriarchy while identifying themselves.

On the whole, therefore, it can be said that the identification pattern of women, just like that of men, shows a considerable hold of patriarchy on them. There are of course a few exceptions in case of both men as well as women.

It has been noted that while choosing the beneficiaries of their donations, men gave preference to parents/mother/father. The other beneficiaries were self, paternal uncle, wife, son, brothers, and in a few cases, daughters and sisters.

In contrast to this, in women's inscriptions, in most of the cases they themselves were the beneficiaries of their donations. Occasionally names of relatives appear as the beneficiaries.

Should we conclude from this that women were more self-centred than men were? Not so, in my opinion. We should look to the sexual division of labour for an explanation of this phenomenon. Sexual division of labour carried different meanings in different times and places. It varied according to different cultural and social settings.[37] In Indian culture, especially urban culture, the most important duty of men was to provide material/financial support to fulfil the needs of their dependents. The needs did not only mean physical needs of clothing, shelter etc., but also included religions and spiritual needs. It is this sense of duty, which probably guided men to donate for the spiritual merit of their relatives.

Women, on the other hand, were expected to look after children, to nurse the sick and old, and to do the household work. They were not expected to support the members of their families financially. This, it seems, is the reason why most of the women did not donate for the benefit of their family members or relatives.

It could be said, therefore, that the manner in which men as well as women chose the beneficiaries of their donations also indicates considerable hold of patriarchy on them.

Most of the men and women donated for objects like images etc., but the donations involving middle level and especially large amounts, like construction of temples, came almost exclusively from men. As men were in control of the financial resources this was only natural.

The majority of the donors, men as well as women, came from the two castes of Shrimala and Pragvata.

**Gender Relations:** Analysis of the inscriptions of this period reveals that the proportion of group donations in which men and women associated with each other is very less, indicating relative independence of men and women in such matters. Kumkum Roy had also noted this phenomenon in her study of Sanchi inscriptions.[38] This suggests that the line demarcating men's and women's spheres of activities was quite clear. That the spheres of activities of men and women were separate is also indicated by the way they chose the beneficiaries of their donations. It has been noted above that men and women acted in accordance with the roles assigned to them. Most men, as providers of financial support, donated for the benefit of their family members. Most women not being required to do so, did not do so.

Men's preference for mothers (also fathers/parents) as the beneficiaries of their donations indicated that mother was the most important woman in their view. Sisters and daughters were married early in life and so did not occupy much space in the men's familial world. The presence of polygamy is attested by the inscriptions, indicating that wives were looked at more as possessions than as life partners.

Only one woman opted for motherly attribute of identity. 43 per cent of the women donors have preferred wifely attribute of identity and 25 per cent have chosen their daughterly attribute. This indicates the relative importance attached by the women to their relationship with husbands and fathers. Only a few women mention brothers and sons in their records.

To sum up, the important observations about the epigraphic sources of Gujarat of this period are:

Firstly, the total absence of the women of Vastupala and Tejapala's family as donors. None of the women of this family figures as donors though they are well represented and find a respectful mention in the records of Vastupala and Tejapala. In fact both the brothers, especially Tejapala, donated for the benefit of all his relatives, except his parents. It is very difficult to give a reason for this. Probably, as the most influential and powerful male members of the family, they took upon themselves the duty of donating for the spiritual merit of all their family members—men as well as women. Anupama and other women of the family, respecting the patriarchal values of their times, let the men do this job while they themselves took a secondary position.

Secondly, patriarchal values also find reflection in the other records of the period.

Thirdly, though most of the women used the set pattern while placing their donations on record. However, they made certain variations in this pattern. For instance, while most of the women used the terms *bharya* or *patni* to indicate their wifely status, Virika prefers the term *pranayini*. Perhaps she wanted to stress that she was the most loved wife of her husband. Similarly, for indicating daughterly status women generally used the term *putri* or *sutaa* or *duhita*. However, a few women have called themselves *putrika*, indicating their legal status as heirs to their father's property. Chahinadevi has preferred her daughter-in-law status to identity herself. Some women used the religious attribute *shravika* or the feminine forms of the professional attributes in addition to their familial attributes. Some others were satisfied with their personal names alone.

Fourthly, the donations involving large sums came, almost exclusively, from men.

Fifthly, there are only a few records in which nuns find mention, whereas monks find mention in almost all records. There is one example where a nun finds mention as a motivator and another one where she is called the preceptor. In addition to this, some sculpted images of nuns have also been noted. These few records in which nuns find mention, attest to the presence of the order of nuns, but they also bring to light the disparity between the status of monks and nuns.

Thus, it can be said that patriarchal values find reflection in most of the women's inscriptions. They use the set pattern to record their donations. However, the slight variations that they make in these records suggest that the women exercised a certain amount of autonomy in the epigraphic space offered to them.

## Notes

1. S.B. Rajyagor, *History of Gujarat* (New Delhi: S. Chand and Company, 1982), p. 108.
2. R. William, *Jaina Yoga* (1963; rpt. Delhi: Motilal Banarasidas Publisher Pvt. Ltd., 1998), p. xii.

3. H.G. Shastri, *A Historical and Cultural Study of the Inscriptions of Gujarat* (Ahmedabad: B.J. Institute of Learning and Research, 1989) p. 144.
4. Ibid., p. 160.
5. Ibid., p. 164.
6. John E. Cort, *Jains in the World, Religious Values and Ideology in India* (New Delhi: Oxford University Press, 2001), p. 38.
7. Bhogilal Sandesara, "Great Hindu Women in Gujarat and Saurashtra", in Svami Madhavananda and R.C. Majumdar (ed.) *Great Women of India* (Advaita Ashram, Himalayas, 1953) p. 365.
8. H.G. Shastri op. cit., p. 164.
9. *PJLS-II*, Inscription no. 64.
10. H.G. Shastri op. cit., p. 165
11. *PJLS-II*, Inscription nos. 38–44, pp. 47–69.
12. *Shat, part 4*, p. 95.
13. Bhogilal Sandesara op. cit., pp. 365–66.
14. The abbreviations for the feminine form of the professional attributes are the same as those for masculine forms.
15. More about this has been explained under the heading 'Women with daughterly attribute' of identity in the same chapter.
16. Though undated, the most likely date of this inscription is V.S. 1378 as the donors are the wives of the donor of the inscription no. 132 of the same source. The monks mentioned in the two inscriptions are also same.
17. *JPLS*, p. 6.
18. U.P. Shah, *Jaina Rupa Mandana (Jaina Iconography)*, (New Delhi: Abhinava Publications,1987), p. 33, 34, 39.
19. H.D. Sankalia, *Studies in the Historical and Cultural Geography and Ethnography of Gujarat*. (Poona: Deccan College, 1949), p. 151.
20. N.N. Bhattacharya, 'Property Rights of Women in Ancient India', in Kumkum Roy (ed.), *Women in Early Indian Societies*, (New Delhi: Manohar Publishers and Distributors, 1999), p. 122.
21. K.M. Munshi, R.C. Majumdar and A.D. Pusalkar, (ed.), *The Struggle for Empire* (Vol. V of the History and Culture of the Indian People Series, 11 Vols., Bombay: Bharativa Vidya Bhavan, 1957), p. 483.

22. P.V. Kane, *History of Dharmashastra III*, pt I (Poona: Bhandarkar Oriental Research Institute, 1941), pp. 345–46.
23. See below, Chapter V, under the heading 'Daughter'.
24. K.K. Shah, *The Problem of Identity: Women in Early Indian Inscriptions* (New Delhi: Oxford University Press, 2001) p. 111.
25. G.V. Devasthali, V.B. Joshi and G.R. Kulkarni, *The Students New Sanskrit Dictionary* (Mumbai: M/s Keshav Bhikaji Dhavale, 1995) p. 639.
26. Some portion of this record is lost. It is quite possible that she had used some familial attribute which has not come down to us.
27. See above Citation no. 11 of 'Women with wifely attribute of identity'.
28. N. Shanta, *The Unknown Pilgrims* (Delhi: Sri Satguru Publications, 1997), p. 178.
29. *Shat,* Inscription no. 54 and 144, pp. 25, 39.
30. K.K. Shah op. cit., p. 153.
31. N. Shanta, loc. cit.
32. See below, Chapter V, under the heading 'Church Administration'.
33. Nalini Balbir, "Women and Jainism in India", in Arvind Sharma (ed.), *Women in Indian Religions*, (New Delhi: Oxford University Press, 2002), p. 92.
34. Munishri Yashoviyayaji, "Jaina Sadhvijioni Bhavya Pashana Pratimao", in Bhogilal Sandesara et al. (ed.) *Acharya Shri Vijaya Vallabha Smaraka Grantha, Gujarati Section*, (Mumbai: Mahavira Jaina Vidyalaya, 1956), p. 172.
35. Ibid.
36. Harihar Sing, "Women's Patronage to Temple Architecture," in Kumkum Roy (ed.), *Women in Early Indian Societies* (New Delhi: Manohar, 1999) p. 294.
37. Vidyut Bhagwat, "The Sexual Division of Labour", in Maithreyi Krishnaraj (ed.), *Contribution to Women's Studies* Series–7, Part II: *Material Base for Subordination,* (Bombay: Research Centre for Women's Studies, SNDT Women's University, 1990), p. 1.
38. Kumkum Roy. "Women and Men Donors at Sanchi: A Study of Inscriptional Evidence", in L.K. Tripathi (ed.) *Position and Status of Women in Ancient* India, Vol. I, 1988, p. 220.

# 3

# Women as Wives

## 15th Century C.E. to 17th Century C.E. (Period II)

During this period Gujarat was under Muslim rule. Upto 1573 it was under Gujarat Sultanate. In the same year Akbar conquered Gujarat and made it a province of the Mughal empire. The Mughal rule lasted up to 1748 C.E.[1] On the whole this was a period of prosperity for Gujarat.[2] Gujarat also produced some famous personalities who left their mark on this era. The first half of the 15th century is known as *Somasundarayuga* in the Jaina history. Somasundara was a prominent monk of this period. With his counsel, the Jainas of Gujarat glorified Jainism. They built new temples, repaired old ones, installed new images of *tirthankaras*, opened libraries, helped the poor and performed many other pious and religious deeds.[3] Many of the Gujarat Jaina merchants maintained good relations with the Muslim rulers. Gunaraja, for instance, was Ahmad Shah's favourite jeweller, and when he went on a pilgrimage to Shatrunjaya in 1420–21 C.E., Ahmad Shah placed his resources at the disposal of Gunaraja to make the pilgrimage a great success.[4] Similarly, Karma Shah, a cloth merchant, who repaired Samra Shah's temple on Shatrunjaya hill in 1531 C.E., had good relations with Bahadhur Shah. Bahadur Shah had given Karma Shah *farman* to repair the temple.[5]

Another prominent Jaina personality of Gujarat was Hirvijayasuri. He become head of the Jaina community in 1566.[6] He was invited by Akbar to attend meetings at *Ibadatkhana*. He created in Emperor Akbar a deep love for the Jaina principles. Hirvijayasuri also succeeded in persuading Akbar to give up the practice of confiscating the property of a deceased childless person. Under his influence, Akbar also abolished *jaziya*.[7] For all these reasons the second half of the 16th century is known as *Hirakayuga*.

Yashovijaya was a prominent *acharya* of the 17th century. He composed several excellent treatises and various valuable commentaries in Sanskrit.[8]

One important event of medieval Gujarat was the religious reform movement in Jainism initiated by a *shravaka* Lokashah of Gujarat, which resulted in the formation of the Sthanakavasi sub-sect of Shvetambaras. Lokashaha had mainly opposed laxities in the conduct of Jaina monks and image worship. Because of this reform movement initiated by Lokashah, Jaina *sadhvis* and *shravikas* got back some of their rights such as discussing religion, giving sermons, etc.[9] Since inscriptions are related to temple and worship, this study is mainly concerned with the Murtipujaka sub-sect of the Shvetambaras. However, whether the reform movements of Lokashah affected the lives of the Murtipujaka Jaina women or not is not clear.

The temple building and repairing activities of the Jainas of Gujarat continued unhindered in the 15th, 16th and 17th centuries. Nearly 50 per cent of the inscriptions collected for this study belong to the 15th century. There is an unusual concentration of inscriptions in this particular century. Shastri, in his study of the inscription of Ahmedabad, notes that the activity of contributing Jaina images increased considerably after the foundation of Ahmedabad in 1411 C.E. This is true particularly for the later half of the 15th century.[10] This unusual concentration of inscription in one century cannot be explained conclusively in view of the decontextualised nature of records. Entering into the socio-economic conditions of the community is hardly possible given the nature of epigraphic sources.

Another feature of the inscriptions of this period is a great increase in group donations, in which men and women, mostly family members, came together to donate. As Table 1 in Chapter 1 indicates in Chapter 1, percentage of group donations for this period is more than fifty. These group donations are of three types:

| | |
|---|---|
| 1. G-Man | Donation by a group headed by a man |
| 2. G-Woman | Donation by a group headed by a woman |
| 3. Family | Donation by a group in which the chief donor is not specified. |

For the analysis of inscriptions, in this chapter, a pattern similar to that followed in the previous chapter has been followed.

## General pattern of men's inscriptions

Men's inscriptions of this period assume a more stereotypical character. Most of the men appearing in these inscriptions identify themselves with reference to their parents. Many a time names of paternal grand parents, or in some cases the lineages, are also given. The other attributes used are the caste and sometimes *gotra,* and the religious attribute *shravaka* or *sushravaka.* Sometimes the place to which the donor belonged is also given.

The most frequently occurring beneficiaries of these donations were parents, father, or mother. The other beneficiaries were the donors themselves, and their brothers, wives, sons, ancestors, and families. In a few cases, we find donations being made for the spiritual merit of daughter or sister.

The people associating for group donations were the members of the patriarchal joint family, i.e., sons, daughters-in-law, grandsons and others. In a few cases, however, fathers associating with daughters or brothers associating with sisters for donations can also be seen.

Donations were made for one or more of the following purposes:

- Building a new temple.
- Undertaking the repairs of existing structures.
- *Devakulikas* or small shrines.
- *Chaturvinshatipattas.*
- Images of *tirthankaras*.
- Images of monks or their *Padukas*.
- Images of *shravaka, shravikas.*
- In addition, a few other items.

Donations for building temples or even for undertaking repair works were very few. The most common object of donation was the image of a *tirthankara*. This seems quite natural as the amount required for building or renovating a temple must have required large amount that only very few could afford.

Most of the inscriptions of this period follow this pattern. However, there are a few inscriptions, which reflect variation from the norm referred to above. Some of these records are cited below:

1. Samvat 1486, Maha su. 5, Thursday; an image of Shri Shantinatha, dedicated by Hansa, son of Sa. Bhoja and his wife Khetalade of Upakesha caste and Aairi gotra; Hansa also being the husband (*pati)* of Sahajalade --- (*RPLS*, 115, Radhanpur)
2. Samvat 1491, Phalguna vadi 5; an image of *muni* Suvarata, dedicated for the merit of self by Maham. Jesa, along with wife Chamku, daughter Raju, her son (*suta*) Shripal; Jesa being the son of Khoka and his wife Khetalade of Shrimali caste --- (*JDSL-II*, 813, Khambat)
3. Samvat 1508, Vaishakh Su. 3; an image of Shri Dharmanatha, dedicated for the merit of self by Jandu, along with wife Chamku, son Hansaraja and sister Sundai; Jandu being the son (*suta*) of San. Naku and his wife Nayanasiri of Pragvata caste --- (*Shat*, 181, Shatrunjaya)
4. Samvat 1511; an image of Shantinatha, dedicated for the merit of mother-father by Sidhanka, Karmi, Saraga, Khamku,

Mahipaka, Lilade, sons and daughters of Shre. Lipaka – Jasmade of Shri. Shrimali caste---, consecrated by --- (*RPLS*, 170, Radhanpur)

5. Samvat 1513; an image of Shri. Vasupujya, dedicated for the merit of his father-in-law (*shwasura*) Shre. Kelhana and his wife Kilhanade by Shre. Aba, along with wife Sampuri, son Hema, Devaraja etc.; Aba being the son (*putra*) of Shre. Mahiraja and his wife Varju of Pragvata caste --- (*JDLS-I*, 1097, Ahmedabad)
6. Samvat 1520, Vaishakh vadi 7, Saturday; an image of Shri Munisuvatasvami, dedicated for the merit of their parents and ancestors by Samdhara and his sister Kalayari, along with Samadhara's wife Tabku and son Deva; Samadhara being the son (*suta*) of Shre. Lampa and his wife Damku, of Vayada caste --- (*RPLS*, 231, Radhanpur)
7. Samvat 1529, Asadha shudi 2, Monday; an image of Shri Shri Shri *muni* Suvratasvami, dedicated for the merit of self by San. Kalu, brother-in-law (*devara*) of Nathi, wife of Vira, son of Gunia --- of Pragvata caste --- (*JDLS-II*, 309, Bharucha)
8. Samvat 1531; an image of Shri Shantinatha, dedicated for the merit of self by Lasha *sushravaka*, along with his sister (*bhagini*) Vamku; Lasha being the son (*putra*) of Vira and his wife Vanu — of Shri Shrimali caste — (*PLS-I*, 442, Palitana).
9. Samvat 1573, Phalguna su. 2, Monday; an image of Shri Vimalanatha, dedicated for the merit of self by Virasingh along with wife Bagu, daughter (*putrika*) and family; Virasingh being the son of Sa. Kheta and his wife Khitu --- of Osvala caste, Shantat *gotra* --- (*JDSL-II*, 70,Vadora)
10. Samvat 1578, Magh vadi 9, Monday; an image of Shri Vimalanatha, dedicated for the merit of his religious sister (*dharmabhagini*) by Maham. Varajanga, along with wife Jivu, son San.Kanha, Man. Megharaja etc.; Varajanga being the son of Maham. Narada and his wife Rangi of Shri Shrimali caste, --- (*JDLSI*, 385,Patan)
11. Samvat 1620, Vaishakha shudi 5; a small shrine (*devakulika*) of Shri Shantinatha, dedicated by Vyo. Samaria of Pragvata

caste, resident of Gandhara along with wife Bai Bholu, daughters Devagai and Bai Kibai, along with family --- (*Shat*, 7, Shatrunjaya)

It has been noted that in the group donations, members of the group were generally the members of a patriarchal family. However, such is not the case in a few records.

In citations (9) and (11) the chief donors are men and their associate donors are their wives and daughters. In (11) Samaria donates with his wife and two daughters. There is no mention of his sons. It is quite probable that he did not have a son. The donor Virsingh of (9), in all probability, was also sonless. He has called his daughter *putrika*—indicating that he was sonless and therefore son hood was ascribed on her.[11] Another inscription similar to this is the citation (2). In this the chief donor Jesa, associates his grandson, the daughter's son with him. (Whether Jesa associated only his grandson or also his daughter is not clear from the phraseology of the record.) While it was quite common to associate one's sons and sons' sons in the donation, associating daughter's son was very rare. Therefore, it is quite probable that Jesa was also sonless and so his daughter and her son Shripala were the heirs of his property. However, as the record is decontextualised, nothing can be said conclusively. The possibility that Jesa associated his daughter's son with him out of pure affection remains. In the records just mentioned above, it seems that daughter's were heirs or inheritors of their father's property. In these records, there is no mention of son-in-law. In fact, in the corpus of inscriptions collected for the study there is not even a single record in which son-in-law finds mention. However, there is one record where a son-in-law has donated for the spiritual merit of his parents-in-law. Aba of citation (5) has donated for the spiritual merit of his in-laws. This is also very rare. Therefore, it is most likely that Aba's wife Sampuri was the only daughter of her parents, and was in place of a son. Along with the right to inherit their property, the duty of taking care of them must also have fallen on her. Which is why her husband donated for their merit. Of course, even here it is quite possible that Aba donated for his in-laws out of respect for them.

Citations (3), (4), (6) and (8) are records in which brothers and sisters have come together to donate, but in each case the position of the sister is different. In (3), Jadu is the chief donor and the associate donors are his wife, son and sister. In (8) Lasa, is the chief donor, while his sister is the only associate donor. In (4) brothers and sisters are co-donors and there is no chief donor, whereas in (6) Kalayri along with her brother Samdhara is the chief donor and Samdhara's wife and son are associate donors. In (3) it seems that her brother Jadu associated Sundai as one of his dependents, while in records (4) and (6) the position of sisters is equal to that of their brothers.

In patriarchy, it is the men who provide identity to women, as fathers, husbands, brothers or sons. The reverse is true very rarely. In the past, sometimes women as mothers have formed a part of men's identity. Even in this collection of inscriptions mothers find mention alongside fathers, as the attribute of men's identity. However, women in any other capacity never form a part of men's identity. Nevertheless, there are two such records. In citation (1), a man uses his wife's name as one of his attributes of identity. Hansa, the donor calls himself son of Bhoja and Bhavalde and husband of Sahajalde. This record comes from Radhanpur and relates to the caste Upakesha. In citation (7) Kalu, the donor, identities himself as the younger brother in-law (*devara*) of Nathi. It is very difficult to say why Hansa and Kalu did so. It could probably be either because of some power equation or out of respect for the women concerned or because of some other reason.

In citation (10), Varajanga, along with his family, donates for the spiritual merit of *shravika* Manju, his *dharmabhagini*. This term has many connotations—a lawful sister, a daughter of a spiritual preceptor, spiritual sister, any one regarded as sister, or one discharging the same religious duties.[12] However, in this place the last meaning seems more appropriate. The donor has probably used the term to indicate that Manju was his co-religionist for whom he had special regard. Manju's religious attribute *shravika* indicates that she was indeed a Jaina.

## Women's inscriptions

There are more than four hundred women's inscriptions of this period. They include the following types:

1. Woman — In which a woman appears as donor.
2. Women — In which two or more women together are the donors.
3. G-Woman — In which donation is made by a group of men and women, and the chief donor is a woman.

For the purpose of analysis they have been classified under the following heads:

1. Women with wifely attribute of identity.
2. Women with daughterly attribute of identity.
3. Women with wifely and daughterly/sisterly attributes of identity.
4. Women with personal name alone.
5. G-Woman inscriptions.
6. Women renouncers.
7. *Sati* inscription.

## Women with wifely attribute of identity

Below are cited a few inscriptions where women have identified themselves as wives. Citations 2, 23 and 25 are lengthy and therefore only relevant portions of these records have been cited.

1. Samvat 1471, Vaishakha sudi 5, ---; a Jina temple (*Jina Prasada*), dedicated by Indrabai, wife (*bharya*) of Shah Shri 5 Manikachanda Panachanda of Shrimali caste, inhabitant of Rajnagara, --- (*Shat*, 138, Shatrunjaya)
2. Samvat 1483, Vaishakha vadi 13, Thursday; a small shrine (*dehari*), dedicated for the merit of self by Khimadevi, wife (*bharya*) of Sa. Khima, son of Sa.Teja and his wife Tejalade of Mithadiya *gotra* --- (*JPLS*, 300, Jiraula)
3. Samvat 1484, Vaishakh vadi 11, Sunday; an image of Shri Shantinatha, dedicated for the merit of self by Saluna *shravika*, wife (*bharya*) of Talha, son of San. Soma and his

wife Sigarade of Shri Shrimali caste, ---. (*RPLS*, 111, Radhanpur)

4. Samvat 1502, Magha vadi 2, Friday; Sambhavanatha *Panchatirthi*, dedicated for the merit of her daughter (*paroksha putrika*) Lakhami by Ladiki, wife (*bharya*) of *gandhi* Mula of Shri Shrimali caste, --- (*JDLS-I*, 230, Patan)
5. Samvat 1511, Ashadha shudi 6, Friday; Shri Shantinatha *Panchatirthi*, dedicated for the merit of her son (*suta*) Saliga and daughter-in-law (*vadhu*) Suhavadevi by Taku *shravika*, wife (*bharya*) of Vya. Shre. Champa --- consecrated by --- (*JDLS-I*, 1160, Patan)
6. Samvat 1513, Magha sudi ... an image of Shri Shantinatha, dedicated for the merit of self by Phatku, wife (*bharya*) of Man. Gola, son of Man. Soma and his wife Jamku of Pragvata caste,--- (*Shat*, 306, Shatrunjaya)
7. Samvat 1517, Vaishakha sudi 12, Monday; an image of *Jivitasvami* Shri Shambhavanatha, dedicated by Puri, wife (*bharya*) of Maham. Deva, son of Mahunasingh and his wife Siriyadevi of Shri Shrimali caste --- (*Shat*, 409, Shatrunjaya)
8. Samvat 1519, Vaishakha vadi 11, Friday; an image of Shri Sambhavanatha, dedicated for the merit of self by Bai Somadevi, wife *(bharya)* of Saha Sahade, son of Sa. Kanahada and his wife Lakhamai of Osvala caste, Shatvada *gotra* --- (*PLS-I*, 335, Jamnagar)
9. Samvat 1521, Posa vadi 1, Thurday; an image of Shri Sumati, dedicated for the merit of self by Gurai, wife (*bharya*) of Hasa Harapati, son of Dosi Varasingha --- consecrated by --- (*Shat*, 244, Shatrunjaya)
10. Samvat 1528, Kartika shu. 13, Saturday; an image of Shri Shri Shri Adinatha, dedicated for the merit of in-laws, husband and self by Himi, wife (*bharya*) of Vagha, son of Shre. Dharana and his wife Phataku of Shri Shrimali caste --- (*RPLS*, 155, Shatrunjaya)
11. Samvat 1528, Phalguna shudi 7; an image of Shri Padmaprabha dedicated by Guri, wife (*bharya*) of Vya.

Mosha, son-in-law (*jamatru*) of San. Bhima and his wife Arghu of Disvala caste, --- (*JDLS-II*, 852)

12. Samvat 1530, Phaguna sudi 7, Wednesday; an image of Sumatinatha, dedicated for the merit of her husband by Ratu *shravika*, wife (*bharya*) of Mahiraja, son of Man. Vela and his wife Valhinade of Shri Shrimali caste --- (*PLS-I*, 431, Jamnagar)
13. Samvat 1530, Magha vadi 2, Friday; an image of Shri Shitalanataha, dedicated for the merit of her mother by Dhanasihi, second wife (*dwitiya bharya*) of Bhrutara, son of Do. Raja and his wife Shemu of Shri Shrimali caste. The first wife of Bhrutara being Rangi --- (*Shat*, 445, Shatrunjaya)
14. Samvat 1531, Maha sudi 10, Monday; an image of Shri *Jivitasvami* Vimalanatha, dedicated for the merit of her husband and for the merit of self by Badaghi, wife (*bharya*) of Sahisa, son of *mantri* Maia and his wife Manikade of Shri Shrimali caste --- (*JDLS-II*, 846, Khambat)
15. Samvat 1535, Magha sudi; an image of Shri Suvidhinatha, dedicated by Mannai *shravika*, wife (*bharya*) of Mahiraja, son of Sa. Ramanalal and his wife Ramade of Ukesha *vamsha*, Balahi *gotra* --- (*RPLS*, 295, Radhanpur)
16. Samvat 1544, Vaishakha sudi 6, Thursday; an image of Shri Shreyansanatha, dedicated for the merit of her family by Ramai, wife (*bharya*) of Sa. Pavayana, son of San. Gola and his wife Duba of Shri Shrimali caste, inhabitants of Shri Anahillapattana --- (*Shat*, 355, Shatrunjaya)
17. Samvat 154, Vaishakha shudi 3, Monday; an image of Shri Sambhavanatha, dedicated for the merit of self by San. Kautigade, wife (*bharya*) of San. Nana, son of Shre. Sarvana and his wife Asu of Kapola caste --- (*PLS-I*, 499, Surat)
18. Samvat 1547; ... a small shrine (*devakulika*), dedicated for the merit of Thobi by Athaku, wife (*bharya*) of Sa. Vejasingh, son of Manaki; Manaki being the daughter of Sa. Mosha and his wife Thobi of Shri Shrimali caste, inhabitants of Shri Stambhatirtha,

or

Samvat 1547; ... a small shrine (*devakulika*), dedicated for the merit of Thobi by Athaku, wife (*bharya*) of Sa. Vejasingh, son of Sa. Mosha and his wife Thobi of Shri Shrimali caste, inhabitants of Shri Stambhatirtha, Vejasingh's sister being Manaki. (*APJLS*, 439, Abu)

19. Samvat 1547, Magha sudi 10, Thursday; an image of *Jivitasvami* Shri Sumatinatha, dedicated for the merit of self by Maniki, wife (*bharya*) of Meha, son of Vya. Kota and his wife Kasmirade of Shri Shrimali caste --- (*RPLS*, 307, Radhanpur)
20. Samvat 1547, Vaishakha vadi 1, Monday; an image of Parshvanatha, dedicated for the merit of self by Manikade, wife (*bharya*) of Man. Manika, son of Man. Jivana of Shri Shrimali caste and his wife Janu --- (*RPLS*, 309, Radhanpur)
21. Samvat 1548, Vaishakha shudi, Thursday; an image of Shri Sheetalanatha, dedicated for the merit of self by Hemade, wife (*bharya*) of Sa. Hemaraja of Pragvata caste, --- (*JDLS-I*, 1155, Radhanpur)
22. Samvat 1617, Posha sudi 13, Monday; an image of Shri Adinatha, dedicated for the merit by Vanade, second wife (*dwitiya bharya*) of Maham. Gela, son of Maham. Narada and his wife Nayakade of Shri Shrimali caste; Maham. Gela's first wife being Ramade --- (*JDLS-I*, 297, Patana)
23. Samvat 1661, Vaishakha sudi 7, Monday; a temple built and image of Mulanayaka Shri Chintamani Parshvanatha set up after spending abundant wealth by Tejalade on the order (*adnya*) given by her husband, *sauvarnika* (goldsmith) Tejapala, son of *sauvarnika* Vacha and his wife Suhasini,--- of Ukesha caste, Abuhara *gotra*, inhabitants of Stambhatirthanagara --- (*HIG-V*, 66, Khambat)
24. Samvat 1677, Va. Margashirsha shudi 5, Sunday; an image of Shri Sumatinatha, dedicated by Bai Putali, wife (*bharya*) of Bhan. Mansangh, son of Bhan. Laxmidhara and his wife Ba Jasade of Osvala caste, *Vriddha shakha*, residents of Shri Pattana --- (*RPLS*, 374, Radhanpur)

25. Samvat 1682, Jyeshtha vadi 9, Thursday; an image of *muni* Suvaratasvami ---, dedicated for the merit of self by Bai Kuvari, wife (*bharya*) of Sa. Sahasakirana of Osvala caste, inhabitant of Ahmedabad, ---. (PJLS-II, 541, Surat)
26. Samvat 1682, Jyeshtha vadi 9, Thursday; an image of Shri Adinatha, dedicated by the wife (*bharya*) of Sa. Shantidasa of Osvala caste, inhabitant of Ahmedabad --- (*PJLS-II*, 542, Surat)
27. Samvat 1683, Ashadha vad 4, Thursday; an image of Shri Neminatha, dedicated by Kapurade, wife (*bharya*) of Karamachand of Ukesha caste, inhabitant of Jalapura ---. (*Shat*, 221, Shatrunjaya)

A vast majority of the women donors of this period, that is more than 70 per cent, identify themselves using their wifely attribute of identity.

Citation (1) is a record of a donation for the Jina temple at Siddhagiri. The donor is *Indrabai*, wife of Panachanda, of Srimali caste. This record is important because it is one of the few records in which women figure as the donors of objects involving large sums. In the previous chapter it has been noted that for period I, there is no epigraphic record of a big donation by women. However, for period II there are a few of records in which women have donated large sums. Record of Tejalade, citation (23) is yet another record where a woman has donated for the construction of a temple. It says that Tejalade, wife of Soni Tejapala, in accordance with the instructions from her husband, donated large sums of money for the construction of a *Jina prasada* or a *Jina* temple at Khambata, their native place. The year of the record is V.S. 1661. Tejalade uses her wifely attribute to identify herself. She has also indicated the caste name *Ukesh*, gotra *Abuhara* and her place of origin.

A big *prashasti* or eulogy of Soni Tejapala from Shatrunjaya[13] may be considered here. It records the renovation of a temple by Tejapala. Karma Shah had renovated this temple only a few years before. The year of Tejapala's record is V.S. 1649. Tejalade also finds mention in this inscription as the beloved wife (*pranayini*) of

Tejapala. The record says that both of them together were enjoying all the luxuries of life like *Indra* and *Indrani*. This description is quite similar to that of the life of the parents of *tirthankaras* by Hemacandra in his TSPC.[14] There are also a few more records of Soni Tejapala. The last one of these is dated V.S. 1659 (*JDLS-II*, 913).

Two things are worth noting in Tejalade's record—first the similarity between the names of husband and wife. Tejapala and Tejalade. A few more records in which names of husband and wife are similar have been noted. For instance, in citation no. (20) and (21), Mnik-Mnikade & Hemrja-Hemade respectively. It seems that sometimes the name of the wife was changed after marriage to suit that of her husband. Some such cases are also noticeable in the Canonical literature. For instance, in *Jnatadharmakatha*, Dhanya *sarthavaha's* wife was Dhanyaa.[15] Such a practice was also current until a few years ago among Hindus of Maharashtra. In both the cases, women were expected to merge their identity in that of their husband's. Changing the name of wife to suit that of the husband must have facilitated the process.

Secondly, the record tells us not only that Tejalade contributed for the construction of a temple but also that she did so in accordance with the instructions from her husband. The wording of this record and the dates of Tejapala's and Tejalde's records suggest that Tejalade had inherited the property of her husband after his death, and was now making the donation to honour his wishes. In the record Tejalade establishes herself as not only the obedient wife but also one who spent her husband's money only for the just cause.

Generally, the *prashastis* are drafted in such a way that the idealised picture of the donor is created. Tejapala's *prashasti* and Tejalade's record, both serve this purpose. The picture of Tejpal that emerges is that of a good shravaka and an ideal husband, and that of Tejalde as a good shravika and an ideal wife. Thus, to that extent, the difference between the epigraphic record and literary sources is blurred.

Donating objects involving large sums was rare for women. However, even the donations involving middle level investment were not many. There are 4 to 5 records where women have donated for *devakulikas* or small shrines. Two such records have been cited. Athaku, the donor of (18) and Khimadevi, the donor of (2) have both contributed for the construction of *devakulikas*. Athaku has identified herself using her wifely attribute. As the phraseology of this inscription is not clear, it could be translated in two ways. According to the first, Athku has probably identified her husband, Vejasingh, with reference to only his mother Manaki and his maternal grand parents Mosa and Thobi. Moreover, Athaku has donated for the spiritual merit of her husband's maternal grandmother, Thobi. The importance given by Athku to her mother-in-law and her parents may be because they were rich and influential people, or may be Manaki, mother-in-law of Athaku, was the only daughter of her parents and had inherited her father's property, or perhaps, it may be out of pure respect for them. The other interpretation of the record could be that Vejasingh was the son of Mosha and Thobi, and Manaki was his sister. Athaku has donated for the merit of her mother-in-law Thobi. However, it seems that the first interpretation is more plausible. This is because mostly the daughters, when they were not the donors, did not find mention.

If Athaku donated for the merit of her grandmother-in-law (or mother-in-law), there is also a record where a woman has made donation for her daughter-in-law. Taku of (5) has donated for the spiritual merit of her daughter-in-law, Suhavadevi. Taku, in addition to her wifely attribute, also uses her religious attribute *shravika*. However, her wifely attribute comes first and then comes her religious attribute *shravika*. Probably for her, being a wife was more important than being a *shravika*. There are a few more women who also used their religious attribute in addition to their wifely attribute. Saluna of (3) Ratu of (12) and Mannai of (15) are some such women. However, in all these cases the religious attribute comes only after their wifely attribute. Of these, Saluna has donated for the spiritual merit of her own self and Ratu has donated for the spiritual merit of her husband. In fact, there were quite a few women of this period, who donated for the spiritual merit of their husbands.

Himi of (10) has donated for the benefit of her in-laws, husband and her own self. Badaghi of citation (14) has donated for the benefit of her husband as well as her own self. In this citation of Badaghi, we find the use of *jivitasvami*. There were also some more women who made use of the term. As has been noted in the previous chapter, probably the *saubhagyavati* women used this term in order to indicate that their husbands were alive at the time of making donations. Alternatively the term may have been used to indicate the iconographic type of the image donated.[16]

Some women of this period donated for the spiritual merit of one of their close relatives. The most preferred beneficiary after one self was the husband. The other beneficiaries being parents, in-laws, sons, daughters and so on. Ramai of (16) has donated for the benefit of her family, while Ladiki of (4) has donated for her daughter. In this record, the term *putrika* has been used for daughter. While analysing the epigraphic records of period I, three or four records in which the term *'putrika'* has been used had been noted. For period II too there are two or three records making use of the term. It has been noted that the term indicated the legal status of the daughter, as the appointed daughter of her father.[17] Normally, daughters could not inherit the property of their fathers. Only in exceptional cases, where the father was sonless, she could be the inheritor of her father's property.

The donor of (11), Guri was also probably the one who had inherited the property of her father. She has identified herself in a very unique way. She has used the wifely attribute, but has identified her husband with reference to her parents, not his. She calls her husband the son-in-law or *jamatru* of Bhima and Araghu.

The epigraphic sources attest the presence of polygamy in the Jaina community of Gujarat. Dhanasihi of (13) and Vanade of (22) have called themselves the second wives of their respective husbands. Dhanasihi has donated for her mother while Vanade has not mentioned the beneficiary of her donation.

Very few women make use of the professional attribute to identify themselves. Kautigade of (17) has used the attribute *sanghvini*, the feminine form of her husband's professional attribute. Probably she took pride in being wife of a *Sanghavi*.[18]

Most women gave their personal names along with their wifely attribute. However, there were few, like the donor of (26), who did not give their personal name. Donor of (26) was the wife of Shantidas of Ahmedabad. Her husband was so famous and well known that being his wife was in itself very prestigious for her. In this record, the donor has not given the names of Shantidasa's parents either. This also indicates that in the donor's opinion Shantidasa needed no other identity. It is possible that this is the same Shantidasa who was the first *nagarshetha* of Ahmedabad by popular voice and was very influential at the imperial court at Delhi.

Somadevi of (8) donated for the image of *Sambhavanatha.* She followed the conventional format to record her donation except that she gave her *gotra* in addition to her caste. Mannai of (15) has also indicated her *gotra.* However there are very few cases in which *gotra* has been indicated.

In records (6), (24), (25) and (27), the donor women have followed the conventional pattern while recording their donations.

## Women with daughterly and/or sisterly attributes of identity

We have seen that a vast majority of the women of this period identified themselves using their wifely attribute of identity. However, approximately 15 per cent identified themselves using their daughterly attribute of identity. In addition, there were also a few women who used their sisterly attribute of identity. Below are cited some inscriptions in which women have identified themselves as daughters/sisters:

1. Samvat 1481, Magha sudi 9, Saturday; an image of Shri *Jivitasvami* Shri Parshvanatha, dedicated by Malhai, daughter (*sutaa*) of Sa. Nagapala and his wife Nagalade of Ukesha vansha, --- (*JDLS-II*, 835, Khambat)
2. Samvat 1489, Phaguna sudi 2, Friday; (*panchatirthi*) dedicated for the merit of her parents by Bai. Dharu, daughter (*putri*) of Shre. Manorasingh and his wife Yamichi of Shri Shrimali caste --- (*Shat*, 416, Shatrunjaya)
3. Samvat 1492, Marga vadi 14, Sunday; a *shikhara*, dedicated for the merit of Sada by Jhamakudevi, daughter (*beti*) of Ada and his wife Ba. Ahavade, inhabitabts of Ghoga. (*JPLS*, 314, Shri Jirapalli)
4. Samvat 1508, Kartika vadi 5; an image of Shri Vasupujya, dedicated for the merit of her husband by Anki, daughter (*sutaa*) of Pata and his wife Hiru. Pata being the son of Maham. Jija of Pragvata caste --- (*JDLS-I*, 840, Ahmedabad)
5. Samvat 1509, Margashirsha sudi 6; an image of Vimalanatha, dedicated by Changai *shravika*, sister (*bhagini*) of Sa. Khima and Sa. Megha, sons of Sa. Naniga of Shrimala vansha and Maghala *gotra* --- (*JDLS-I*, 258, Chani)
6. Samvat 1509, Jyeshtha vadi 9, Thursday; an image of Shri Shantinatha, dedicated for the merit of her parents by Gadi, daughter (*sutaa*) of Man. Kurasi and his wife Kutigade; Kurasi being the son of Man. Saranga and his wife Ba. Sampuri of Osvala caste --- (*JDLS-II*, 401, Nadiad)
7. Samvat 1512; an image of Shri Vasupujya, dedicated by Arghu, sister (*bhagini*) of Pa. Hapa, son of Shre. Kama and his wife Bholi of Pragvata caste --- (*RPLS*, 183, Radhanpur)
8. Samvat 1514, Phaguna sudi 10, Monday; an image of Shri Kunthunatha, dedicated for the merit of self by Sadhu, daughter (*putri*) of Vya. Sa.Karmasi and his wife Rupini of Upakesha caste; their son being Amara --- (*PLS-I*, 295, Jamnagar)

9. Samvat 1515, Ashadha vadi 1; an image of Shri Ajitanatha, dedicated by Devasiri, daughter (*putri*) of Brahman Susharma --- Devasiri (*APJLS*, 500, Abu)
10. Samvat 1529, Maha sudi 9, Saturday; an image of *muni* Suvratasvami, dedicated for the merit of self by Jivini, daughter (*sutaa*) of Do. Champa and his wife Arghu of Shri Humbada caste; Jivini also being the sister (*bhagini*) of Do. Ubha, (wife Bhali). (*RPLS*, 246, Radhanpur)
11. Samvat 1529, Jyeshtha vadi 1, Friday; a *panchatirthi* of Shri Sambhavanatha, dedicated by Putali, daughter (*sutaa*) of Saha. Bhima and his wife Mataku of Shri Pragvata caste, their sons being Dungara, Devaraja etc. ---. (*JDLS-II*, 1141, Khambat)
12. Samvat 15--; a *saptatirthankarapatta*, dedicated for the merit of self by Sanghavini Champai, daughter (*sutaa*) of San. Nesa and his wife Jasmade; Nesa being the son of --- of Osvala caste, inhabitant of Shri Mandava ---, Sanghavini Champai (*PJLS-II*, 130. Abu)
13. Samvat 1567, Magha sudi 5, Thursday; an image of Shri. Chandraprabhu, dedicated for the merit of her husband Kadua by Jivi *shravika*, daughter (*putri*) of Shre. Gunapati and his wife Manu of Shri vansha --- (*JDLS-II*, 222, Vadodara)
14. Samvat 1579, Vaishakh sudi 6, Monday; an image of Shri Shantinatha, dedicated by Bai Vimalai, daughter (*sutaa*) of Shre. Harsha and Maniki of Shri Shrimali caste --- (*RPLS*, 339, Radhanpur)
15. Samvat 1632, Magha sudi 10, Wednesday; Shri Shantinatha *chaturvinshatiptta*, dedicated by Bai Hirai, daughter (*putri*) of Thakar Jaga and his wife Bai Thakarani of Modha caste --- (*JDLS-II*, 668, Khambat)
16. Samvat 1660, Vaishakha shu. 13; an image of Shri Sambahavanatha, dedicated by *shravika* Vira, daughter (*putri*) of *shra*. Vimalade of Shri Shrimali caste --- (*JDLS-II*, 757, Khambat)

The terms used for indicating daughterly status were *sutaa* and *putri*. In one case, we find *beti* being used for this purpose. In citation (3), Jhamkudevi calls herself *beti* of Ada and Bai Ahavade. She has contributed for the construction of a *shikhara*. All those women who identified themselves as daughters were necessarily not unmarried. In case of a few women at least, there is evidence to show that they were married and yet chose to identify themselves as daughters. For instance, Amki of (4) and Jivi (13) have donated for the spiritual merit of their respective husbands. Obviously, they were married and yet identified themselves as daughters. They have not given any other information about their husbands except their personal names. Jivi in addition to her daughterly status also gives her religious attribute *shravika*. However, her daughterly attribute come first and then comes her religious attribute indicating her preference for the daughterly attribute. Mahi of (1) was also probably a married woman. She has used the term *jivitasvami*, which, as noted in the previous chapter, was probably used by the *saubhagyavati* women, the women whose husbands were alive at the time of making donation. However, it is also possible that the term was used to indicate that her parents were alive at the time of making donation, as a few men have done,[19] or else to indicate the iconographic type (see Chapter 1).

In contrast to the women using their daughterly attribute of period I, women of period II generally used their daughterly attribute with reference to both the parents. Nevertheless, Devasiri of (9) has identified herself with reference to her father alone. Devasiri was the daughter of a *brahman* Susharma. However, whether she herself was a Jaina, non-Jaina, or married to a Jaina, is not clear. This inscription is from Abu, where there are a few more inscriptions in which the donors were non-Jainas.[20] As Devasiri was a woman, it is quite possible that she was married to a Jaina and came along with her family for pilgrimage. However, it looks that she took pride in calling herself the daughter of a *brahman*. In identifying herself, she seems to have been guided more by self-perception rather than the social norms. In contrast to the above cases, there is one record where the donor woman has identified herself with reference to her mother alone. Vira of (16) first gives the name of her caste, then the name of her mother along with her *shravika* status. Next she gives her own religious attribute *shravika,* and in the end, she gives her personal name. Whether Vira was married or not is not clear. Nevertheless, the fact that she has not given the name of her father indicates that she, like Devasiri, was also guided by self-perception rather than social norms while constructing her identity. It seems that she was a religious woman for whom being a *shravika* was very important. She took pride in calling herself the daughter of a *shravika*. Besides, it seems that she was probably more influenced by the personality of her mother.

As noted above, many women who identified themselves using the wifely attribute, donated for the spiritual merit of one of their relatives. However, of the women using their daughterly attribute, very few donated for the benefit of their relatives. Anki of (4) and Jivi of (13) donated for the spiritual merit of their husbands, whereas Bai Dharu of (2) Gadi of (6) donated for their parents.

In some records, there is mention of the professional attributes of the donors. For instance Champai of (12), after mentioning her daughterly status, gives her professional attribute, the feminine form of her father's professional attribute, *sanghavi*. The importance attached to the title *sanghavini* by Champai becomes clear when we note that the words *sanghavini* Champai being engraved again at the end of the record. The other record where the feminine form of the professional attribute has been used is the citation (15). In this record the donor Hirai does not take the professional attribute herself, but calls her mother *thakarani*. In fact, she does not even give the personal name of her mother. It may be that Hirai's husband was not a *thakkura* so she did not take the title herself.

Changai of (5) and Arghu of (7) have identified themselves using their sisterly attributes. Changai has mentioned the name of her father but only as the attribute of her brothers' identify. Similarly, Arghu has given the names of her parents, not as the attribute of her own identity, but as that of her brother's identity.

Of the two women, Changai also takes the religious attribute *shravika*. In the above cases, where women chose their sisterly attribute, it seem, that they did so because their brothers, and not their fathers, were at the helm of the family affairs, or that their brothers were more influential. Sadhu of citation (8) and Putali of (11) have, it seems, in addition to the names of their parents, also given the names of their brothers. Though they have identified themselves as daughters, they probably felt that their identity would be incomplete without the mention of their brothers. Jivini of (10) has drafted her record very carefully and identified herself by using both daughterly as well as sisterly attributes of identity. In fact she has gone a step further and has made a mention of her sister-in-law, her *bhabhi*, as well.

Vimalai of (14) has recorded her donations in a conventional manner, without making any variation in the set pattern.

## Women with two-fold familial attributes

Below are cited some inscriptions where women have used their two-fold familial attributes, wifely as well as daughterly. However, citations (5) and (9) being lengthy, only relevant portions of these records have been cited.

1. Samvat 1487, Magha vadi 8, Monday; a *panchatirthi* image of Shri. Vasupujya, dedicated by Amku, wife (*bharya*) of Manor, son of Do. Munja and his wife Malhanade of Shri Shrimali caste, inhabitants of Ghoga; Amku also being the daughter (*putri*) of Sa. Ambada and Ahivade --- (*PLS-I*, 141, Jamnagar)
2. Samvat 1505; an image of Shri Adinatha, dedicated for the merit of her son Natha by Dharpu, wife (*bharya*) of Shiva, son of Do. Sanga and his wife Singarade of Vamiya Pragvata caste; Dharpu also being the daughter (*putri*) of Shre. Duda and Devalade --- (*JDLS-II*, 46, Vadodara)
3. Samvat 1508, Vaishakha shudi 3; an image of Shri Neminatha, dedicated for the merit of self by Jhabaku, wife (*bharya*) of Man. Goinda, son of Pra. Shre. Bhima and his

wife Vabu; Jhabaku also being the daughter (*putri*) of Shre. Champa and his wife Rupi --- (*JDLS-I*, 809, Ahmedabad)

4. Samvat 1524, Vaishakha shudi 2, Monday; an image of Shri Vasupujya, dedicated with the advice of Shri Jayakesrisuri---, for the merit of her mother and father by Rambhalade *shravika*, daughter (*putri*) of Shre. Vachha and his wife Puri of Shri vansha, inhabitants of Hadala village; Rambhalade also being the wife (*bharya*) of Man. Sahasa, son of Man. Hira and his wife Vachu --- (*JDLS-I, 899*, Ahmedabad)
5. Samvat 1525, Phalguna sudi 7, Saturday; an image of Shri Shitalanatha ---, dedicated by a *shravika*, wife (*bharya*) of the king of kings (*rajadhiraja*) Shri Ramdasamanya Man. Sundara, son of Man. Madan, who is like an ornament of Gurjara caste (*gurjarajnatishrungara*) and his wife Loli; The donor is also the daughter (*putri*) of Do. Ratna and his wife Jivini --- (*PJLS-II*, APJLS, 410, Abu)
6. Samvat 1531, Vaishakh vadi 11, Monday; a *chaturvinshatipatta* of Shri Chandraprabha etc., dedicated for the merit of her mother by Ba. Sobhagini, daughter (*putri*) of Sa.Latkana and his wife Karmai --- of Shri Shrimali caste; Sobhagini being also the wife (*patni*) of Sa. Shripati --- (*PLS-I*, 441, Talaja)
7. Samvat 1537, Posha sudi 9, Sunday; an image of Shri Shantinatha, dedicated for the merit of self by Manakai, daughter (*sutaa*) of Sa. Bhoja of Shri. Shrimali caste; Manakai being also the wife (*kalatra*) of Sa. Mahanatha, --- (*Shat*, 236, Shatrunjaya)
8. Samvat 1587, Va. Sha. 1452, Posh vadi 6, Sunday; an image of Shri Ajitanatha, dedicated for the merit of self by Naku, daughter (*putri*) of Shre. Harsha and his wife Aji of Osh vansha, *Laghu shạkha*. On her in-laws side, Naku being the wife (*bharya*) of Man. Hapa, son of Man. Singha --- (*JDLS-II*, 383, Nadiad)
9. Samvat 1706, Jyeshtha vadi 3,Thursday; an image of Shri. Parshvanatha ---, dedicated by *shravika* Naringade, whose fame has become immortal because of her virtue of charity

(*dana*), whose nature is befitting because of her praiseworthy deeds, and who is the daughter (*sutaa*) of Gan. Sura and his wife Lilai of Shri Shrimali caste, *Vriddha shakha*, inhabitants of Shri. Stambhatitrtha; Naringade is also the wife (*vanita*) of Nemidasa, whose limbs are decorated, as if by ornaments, as he possesses all the virtues of a *shravaka*, whose fame has become sweet like the pot of nectar because of his support to the religious deeds of different kind; Nemidasa being the son of Do. Jivaraja --- and his wife Rajabai, as well as nephew of Pari. Vajia-Rajia & Avha (?), who have raised Nemidasa as their own son (*palitaputra*) --- (*JDLS-II*, 561, Khambat)

In a few inscriptions, women have expressed their two-fold identity—as wives as well as daughters. In some of these records we find the daughterly attribute coming before the wifely attribute, while in others the reverse is the case. This indicates the relative importance given to the wifely and daughterly attributes. Most of them express their daughterly status with reference to both the parents. Only a few, like Manakai of citation (7), have given their daughterly status only with reference to their father. Manakai uses the word *kalatra* for indicating her wifely status, Naringade likes the term *vanita*, while most of the other women prefer *bharya or patni*.

Out of the women using their two-fold identity, very few have donated for the spiritual merit of their relatives. Rambhalade of (4) has donated for the spiritual merit of her parents, whereas Sobhagini of (6) has donated for the benefit of her mother. Dharapu of (2) has donated for the spiritual merit of her son.

A few women have, used their religious attribute *shravika* apart from their two familial attributes. The religious attribute generally comes only after daughterly as well as wifely attributes. It sometimes comes before the personal name, like in the case of *shravika* Narigade, or else comes after the personal name like in the case of Rambhalade *shravika*. The donor of citation (5) has not given her personal name at all. She has first given her wifely attribute, then her daughterly attribute, and in the end, her religious attribute. She was the wife of minister Sundara. Minister Sundara and his son, minister Gada, repaired the Bhimashah temple *Pitalahara* on mount Abu in V.S. 1525. They, along with their family, also contributed towards the principal image of Adinatha in the temple. This image was made of brass and other metals.[21] The wife of Sundara does not give her personal name. As her husband was a famous minister, she probably felt it sufficient to call herself his wife. She has contributed a Shantinatha image.

One record, which is different from the rest, is that of Naringade (citation 9). She has first given her daughterly status and then her wifely status using the term *vanita* for this purpose. Though she has first given her daughterly and then her wifely attribute, it does not seem that her wifely attribute was less important for her. On the contrary, while her parents find just a mention, a lot of details about her husband have been given. Her husband Nemidasa, has been identified not only with reference to his parents but also with reference to his maternal uncles. Nemidasa has been called as the *palitaputra* of his maternal uncles, the one who has been brought up by them. Recognising this fact, Narigade has given the same respect to them as she has given to her in-laws. Further Nemidasa and Narigade both have been eulogised and their religious nature has been stressed.

Thus, though Narigade has used the set pattern for recording her donation, she has also provided us with important additional information. She has thoughtfully provided the contents of the record and made good use of the epigraphic space available to her.

**Donors with personal name alone**

1. Samvat 1517, Magha sudi 10, Wednesday; an image of Shri Sumatinatha, dedicated for the merit of self by *shravika* Stu, of Koranta *gaccha*, Upakesha caste and Kalaparamara branch --- (*PLS-I*, 305, Jamnagar)
2. Samvat 1595, Magha vadi 2, Wednesday; an image of Shri Parshvanatha, dedicated by Bai Karamai --- (*JDLS-II*, 453)

3. Samvat 1613, Vaishakha sudi 10, Thursday; an image of Shri Shri Adinatha, son of *Maharaja* Nabhinareshwar, the king of kings, and mother Marudevi, dedicated for *karmakshaya* by Bai Ninu of Shri Shrimali caste and inhabitant of Shri Thiradra. (*JPLS*, 117, Tharad)
4. Samvat 1617, Jyeshtha sudi 5, Monday; an image of Shri Neminatha, dedicated by Bai Kama, consecrated by Shri Vijayadanasuri. (*JDLS-I*, 1102, Ahmedabad)
5. Samvat 1677, Margashirsha sita 5, Sunday; at Stambhatirtha an image of Shri *muni* Suvratasvami, dedicated by *shravika* Nayani --- (*JDLS-II*, 1022, Khambat)
6. Samvat 1677, Kartika sita 6, Sunday; at Stambhatirtha, an image of Anantanatha dedicated for her fame by Hana *shravika* of Modha caste, --- (*JDLS-II*, 379, Khambat)
7. Samvat 1687, Margashirsha sudi 4; an image of Shri Sumatinatha, dedicated by *shravika* Rajimani --- (*RPLS*, 379, Radhanpur)

Just a few women have identified themselves without using any familial attribute. They have used one or more of the following attributes for identifying themselves—caste, place of origin and religious status. The proportion of such women is negligible in the 15th century, whereas it is little more in 16th and 17th centuries. Most of them have either donated for the benefit of themselves or have not mentioned the beneficiary of their donation at all.

Though these inscriptions are brief, it cannot be said that the donor avoided giving their familial attribute to save the engraving space, as they have provided some other details like caste, place etc., and also the details of the monks who consecrated the image. Citation (3), *Bai* Ninu's record is a little different. She gives the names of the parents of Shri Adinatha, the *thirthankara*, whose image she is donating, with their titles. She also gives the caste and place to which she belongs, but does not give her familial attribute, nor does she give the name of the monk who consecrated the image.

Thus, it seems that for these women, whose wife or daughter they were was less important. For them their other attributes were more important. This suggests a greater role of self-perception in their identity formation.

## G-Woman inscriptions

Group donations are a peculiar feature of the Gujarat Jaina inscriptions of this period. Nearly half of the total inscriptions of this period are group donations. In some of these group donations, women are the chief donors. They are the chief donors in nearly 115 group donations. That comes to about more than a quarter of the total women's inscriptions of this period. The structure of most of these has many features in common:

1. The donors first give their caste name, next the lineage of the husband's or the father's family, and then their familial attribute, followed by their personal name. Some donors indicate their religious attribute also. The place to which they belonged is also indicated by some donors. It is given either in the beginning or at the end of the record.
2. Most of them donate for the religious merit of themselves. A few donate for the religious merit of one of their relatives like parent, husband etc. However, it is quite possible that the term *svashreyartham* in a group donation stands for—'the merit of all the donors'.
3. The associate donors were usually their sons and their families. But we also come across such G-Woman inscription in which daughters, brother-in-law, brothers, sisters, co-wives, nephews etc. were the associate donors.
4. Generally, husbands did not become the associate donors though in G-Man inscriptions, wives were nearly always the associate donors. Initially it seemed that probably the women donors became head of their families after the death of their husbands and so husbands did not become the associate

donors. Nevertheless, when I came across a set of three inscriptions belonging to the same family, I realised that such was not always the case. Many a time husbands were alive yet did not form a part of the group. The three inscriptions are those of minister Sundar and his family members. The first inscription is dated V.S. 1525 and the donors were minister Sundar and his son, minister Gada. The associate donors were Sundar's wife, Gada's wife, and Gada's sons. The second inscription is of Sundar's wife alone, having the same date. The third inscription is a group donation by Gada's wife Asu, and her sons. This inscription too is of the same date. Thus Asu made a donation in her own name and associated her sons but did not associate her husband, who was very much alive at the time.[22]

Similarly, the parents of the donor (both men and women), did not become the associate donors. Rarely though, the mother could be the associate donor when her son was the chief donor. Thus, it seems that the familial hierarchy was observed while associating donors in a group donation.

5. Most of the women chief donors of group donations identified themselves using their wifely attributes. Some of them identified themselves using the daughterly attribute, while a few gave both the attributes.

Below are cited some of the G-Woman inscriptions. Wherever the inscriptions are lengthy, only the relevant portion has been cited:

1. Samvat 1482, Phaguna shudi 3, Sunday; an image of Shri Adinatha, dedicated for the merit of self by Singarade, along with her sons, San. Teja, Talha, Hema; Singarade being the wife (*bharya*) of San. Soma of Shri Shrimali caste --- (*RPLS*, 106, Radhanpur)
2. Samvat 1499, Vaishakha vadi 5; an image of Shri Abhinandana, dedicated for the merit of her husband by Hamiradevi, along with her daughter Avikarmai; Hamiradevi being the wife (*bharya*) of Bhan. Pethada of Ukesha vansha, inhabitant of Pattana --- (*JDLS-I*, 368, Patan)

3. Samvat 1495, Jyeshtha vad 6; an image of *muni* Suvrata, dedicated for the merit of self by Jasu, along with her son Nalu; Jasu being the daughter (*putri*) of Shre. Saga and his wife Tilaku --- of Disvala caste ---; her brother Dha. Rajaka and nephews Rana. Kuranala Samala. (*JDLS-I*, 83, Chaveli)
4. Samvat 1500 Vaishakha shudi 5; an image of Shri Vardhamana, dedicated for the merit of self by Phadu, along with her younger brother-in-law (*devara*) Pan. Dhanatili, his sons Vaija, Tira etc.; Phadu being the wife (*bharya*) of Pa. Karmasi of Pragvata caste --- (*RPLS*, 133, Radhanpur)
5. Samvat 1508, Magha shudi 5, Monday; an image of *Jivitasvami* Shri. Sumatinatha dedicated for the merit of self by Madoari, along with her son Soma; Madoari being the wife (*bharya*) of Hatisanga of Ukesha caste --- (*JDLS-I*, 827, Ahmedabad)
6. Samvat 1508, Va. Jyeshtha shu. 9, Wednesday; an image of Shri Shitalanatha, dedicated for the merit of self by Man. Phaku *sushravika* along with her family; Man.Phaku *sushravika* being the wife (*bharya*) of Saranga, (son of) Man. Karana of Pragvata vansha, and his wife Puja, another wife of Karana being Taru; --- (*RPLS*, 152, Radhanpur)
7. Samvat 1508, Ashadha shudi 2, Monday; an image of Shri Shitalanatha, dedicated by Rohini, along with her brothers Jaran etc.; Rohini being the sister (*bhagini*) of Do. Joga, Dhadasi, sons of Do. Dhirana and his wife Hiru of Osvala caste, inhabitants of Ahmedabad --- (*JDLS-I*, 1217, Ahmedabad)
8. Samvat 1509, Margashirsha shudi; an image of Shri Shambhavanatha, dedicated for the merit of self by Valhade *shravika* along with her younger brothers-in-law (*devara*) Sa. Hema, Sa. Deva and their wives Matku and Devasiri respectively, as well as the other family members; Valhade *shravika* being the wife (*bharya*) of Sa. Sada, son of Sa. Sarvana and his wife Tibu, --- of Shri Shrimali caste --- (*JDLS-I*, 994, Ahmedabad)

9. Samvat 1510, Phalguna shudi 11, Saturday; an image of *Jivitasvami* Shri Shantinatha, dedicated for the merit of self by San. Lashu, along with her son Mula; San. Lashu being the wife (*bharya*) of San. Vira, son of San. Devaita and his wife Karmade of Shri Shrimali caste --- (*JDLS-II*, 964, Khambat)
10. Samvat 1512, Margashirsha vadi 15, Monday; an image of *jivitasvami* Shri. Vasupujya, dedicated for the merit of her husband and herself by Maku, along with her son Aana; Maku being the wife (*bharya*) of Man. Mala of Shri Shrimali caste --- (*JDLS-I*, 105, Chanasma)
11. Samvat 1512, Jyeshtha vadi 1; an image of Shri Sumatinatha, dedicated by *shravika* Rajai, along with her brothers San. Harapati, Badua and Varajanga; *shravika* Rajai being the daughter (*sutaa*) of Shan. Narapala of Gurjara caste, inhabitant of Vadali, and his wife Buti. The donor is also the wife (*bharya*) of Man. Godha --- (*JDLS-I*, 1167, Ahmedabad)
12. Samvat 1515, Vaishakha vadi 2, Thursday; *Jivitasvami* Shri Adinatha *chaturvinshatipatta* dedicated for the merit of ancestors as well as self by Mahingaladevi, along with her son Vaula; Mahingaladevi being the wife (*bharya*) of Mokala, son of Isara and his wife Rajalade --- of Shri Shrimali caste --- (*JPLS*, 36, Tharad)
13. Samvat 1521, Vaishakha vadi 2, Thursday; an image of Shri Adinatha, dedicated for the merit of self by *shravika* Lilai daughter (*sutaa*) of Hiru, along with her family-Man. Surasi of Osa vansha, his wife Hiru, their son Man. Singha, his wife Dhani, another son Man. Megha, his wife Kapurai, their sons Nagaraja, Shivadasa --- (*JDLS-II*, 587, Khambat)
14. Samvat 1521, Vaishakha vadi 6, Wednesday; an image of Shri Dharmanatha dedicated for the merit of self by Khimai, along with her son Harischandra and his wife Kikibai; Khimai being the wife (*bharya*) of Bha. Sangrama of Upakesha caste --- (*JDLS-I*, 14, Dabhoi)
15. Samvat 1522, Phaguna shudi 3, Monday; an image of Shri Kunthunatha, dedicated for the merit of self, with the advice

of Jayakesari *suri*, head of Shri. Anchala *gaccha*, by Shrungarade *sushravika*, along with her whole family; Shrungarade being the religious daughter (*dharmaputri*) of Sa. Pasa and his wife Valhade --- (*JDLS-I*, 1290)

16. Samvat 1522, Kartika vadi 1; an image of Shri Adinatha, dedicated for the merit of self by Somi, along with her son Mala, daughter Dahi and the family members; Somi being the wife (*bharya*) of Ratnasi, son of Shre. Dhanapala and his wife Lilade of Shri Shrimali caste --- (*JDSL-II*, 293, Bharuch)
17. Samvat 1523, Phaguna shudi 8 Wednesday; an image of Shri. Vimalanatha, dedicated for the merit of self by Pahuti, along with her husband (*bhartru*) Varajanga; Pahuti being the daughter (*sutaa*) of Sa. Ratna and his wife Puri of Shrimali caste --- (*JDLS-I*, 289, Patan)
18. Samvat 1530, Va. Magha shudi 4, Friday; an image of Shri Neminatha, dedicated for the merit of self by Jhatku, along with her nephew (*bhratruvya*) Kala and other family members; Jhatku being the wife (*bharya*) of Vya. Lala, son of Ramasi and his wife Somi of Pragvata caste, inhabitants of Sambosana --- (*JDLS-II*, 745, Khambat)
19. Samvat 1534; an image of Shri Neminatha, dedicated for the merit of her husband by Kapuri, along with her son Shre. Tisala, his wife Maniki and family; Kapuri being the wife (*bharya*) of Shre. Depala of Shri Shrimali caste --- (*RPLS*, 290, Radhanpur)
20. Samvat 1543; an image of Shri Kunthunatha, dedicated for the merit of her husband by Sakhi, along with her daughter (*putri*) Nathi and her son Yusa; Sakhi being the wife (*bharya*) of Man. Samala, son of Man. Rama and his wife Chamku of Gurjara caste; --- (*JDLS-I*, 1283, Ahmedabad)
21. Samvat 1546, Posha vadi 5, Monday; an image of Shri Parshvanatha, dedicated for the merit of self by Muli *sushravika*, along with son Su. Mandalika and family; Muli being the wife (*bharya*) of *sugandhi* Vachayana of Shri Shri vansha, --- (*Shat*, 198, Shatrunjaya)

22. Samvat 1566 ... shudha 5, Monday; an image of Shri Adinatha, dedicated for the merit of her mother by Purai, along with her sons, Manka, Man. Narasingha, Man. Shridatta and family; Purai being the daughter (*putri*) of Vya. Raja and his wife Nathi --- inhabitants of Stambhatirtha --- (*JDLS-II*, 545, Khambat)
23. Samvat 1572, Chaitra vadi 3; an image of Shri Dharmanatha, dedicated for the merit of self by Jivini *shravika*, along with sons-San. Nakara, San. Dhanapala, grandsons—Rupa, Suta, Kanha and family; Jivini being the wife (*bharya*) of San. Devadatta, son of San. Phugha and his wife *shravika* Kapurade of Ukesha vansha, Chajeda *gotra*; --- (*RPLS*, 330, Radhanpur)
24. --- Samvat 1579, Vaishakha vadi 1, Thursday, an image of Shri Neminatha, dedicated for the merit of self by Karmi *sushravika*, along with brother Bhima and sister Demi; Karmi being the daughter (*putri*) of Megha and his wife Padmai of Shri Shri vansha. The donor is also the wife (*bharya*) of Do. Sihapa --- (*JDLS-I*, 221, Patan)
25. Samvat 1597, Chaitra sudi 13, Thursday; at Pattananagara, at Shri Nishapataka, a *panchatirthi*, dedicated for the merit of Shri *Sangha* by all the Shri *shravikas* --- (*JDLS-I*, 131, Chanasma)
26. Samvat 1677, Kartikà Krishna 2, Wednesday; at Stambhatirtha, an image of Shri Anantanatha, dedicated by *shravika* Shrungarade, along with her first co-wife Bai Shivade, Shivade's daughter Bai Dhanai and second co-wife Valhade; Shringarade being the wife (*bharya*) of Sa. Shrimalla of Osvala caste, *Vriddha shakha*. The donor is also the mother of Sa. Rahia --- (*JDLS-II*, 1058, Khambat)
27. --- Samvat 1683, Magha shukla 13, Monday; renovation of the Jina temple of Chandraprabhasvami, done at the behest of *ubhayakulanandadayini paramashravika* Hirabai, along with her son *parikha* Somachandra and family; Hirabai being the sister (*bhagini*) of Sa. Shri Rupaji, son of Sa. Shrivanta and his wife, *ubhayakulanandadayini* Bai Shri Sobhagade — of Ahmedabad. Hirabai undertook 99 pilgrimages to

Shatrunjaya *tirtha* along with the *sangha*. On her husband's side, she being the wife *(bharya)* of *parikha* Rahia, son of *parikh* Kuaraji (wife Kamalade), son of *parikh* Gunidasa (wife Gurade). Rahia is also the brother of *parikha* Viraji. Also, an image of Shri Chandraparabha *tirthankara* dedicated in the name of her son *parikh* Somachandra, by Hirabai, along with her daughter, Bai Kalyani, brother Rupaji and nephew Gunidasa --- (*Shat*, 25, Shatrunjaya)

28. Samvat 1686, Chaitra shudi, Thursday; a small shrine (*devakulika*), dedicated by Bai Sajanadevi, along with the sons of Harshamade, Man. Jetha, Man. Rupa, and the family members; Sajanadevi being the wife of Man. Rishabhadasa, --- of Shrimali caste --- (*Shat*, 504, Shatrunjaya)

Most of the citations fit into the pattern given above. However, there are a few inscriptions, which need more explanation.

It has been noted that in the group donations familial hierarchy was observed and the seniority of the husbands over their wives was emphasised. A woman generally associated her sons and daughters-in-law, and sometimes daughters, for instance citation no. (2) and (16). Occasionally she also associated her brothers and sisters, like in citations (7), (11), (13) etc. At times a younger brother-in-law *(devara)* could also become her associate donor. However, her husband, in-laws or parents could never become her associate donors, though she identified herself with reference to them. Nevertheless, in citation no. (17) these norms were not observed. In this record, Pahuti, who used only her daughterly attribute of identity, and is the chief donor, associated her husband in her donation. Though it is clear that she has made a variation from the norm but why she did so is difficult to ascertain. The reasons could be many and because of the decontextualised nature of our source, it is difficult to say which one was the true reason. It is quite possible that she was the only daughter of her parents and was heir to their property and her husband may have been financially dependent on them or else was a *gruha jamata* (son-in-law residing in his in-laws' house). Generally, in the past, men had more power than women did, but in a situation like this, the power relations might have been reversed and so were the norms of conduct. There is also a possibility that there was a good understanding between husband and wife and the husband willingly agreed to be an associate donor.

Another record, though different from the above record, could be cited in this context. This is a record of a man who calls himself a *dauhitra* or the daughter's son of Vacha and Paratu and has donated for their (his maternal grand parents) merit.

> Samvat 1509, Jyeshtha vadi 9, Friday; an image of Shri Vasupujya, dedicated for the merit of *saugandhika thakura* Vacha and his wife Partu by their daughter's son (*dauhitrika*) Manika --- (*JDLS-II*, 203, Vadodara)

In this record also there is a possibility that Manika's mother was the only daughter of her parents and therefore Manika was heir to their property or had actually inherited their property. Alternatively this could also be an expression of pure love and respect by Manika for his maternal grandparents. May be he did so at the request of his mother or else, may be he was brought up by them instead of his own parents.

Citation no. (27) is also an important record. Hirabai, the donor, is one of the very few women who have donated for the renovation of the temple. Another important aspect of this inscription, which is a long eulogy, is that the eulogy emphasised on the achievements of Hirabai's natal family, though her husband's family also finds mention. The epithet—*ubhayakulanandadayini*, the woman who brings happiness to both the families—her natal family and her husband's family, is used for her mother and for herself. We are told that Hirabai belongs to the 6th generation of the *mantrishwara* Bhandari, who had constructed the temple at Shatrunjaya. She, in association with her son, contributed for the renovation of the temple. She also donated an image of *tirthnkara* Chandraprabhasvami in the name of her son Somacandra. The eulogy suggests that probably Hirabai derived her prestige from her natal family, of which she was justly proud.

Citations (25) and (26) are such records in which all the donors, including the chief donor, were women. The donor of citation (26), Shrungarade, who identifies herself as wife as well as mother, has associated her two co-wives and a stepdaughter with her. In the patriarchal societies polygamy was common among at least the rich people. It was expected of the co-wives that they maintain harmonious relations. The donors of this record seem to fulfil such an expectation. Few such records have also been noted in period I. Citation (25) tells us that at Pattananagara, or Patan, a group of *shravikas* collectively donated *panchatirthapatta*. Though this is the only record of period II in which a group of *shravikas* coming together to donate can be seen, it is quite possible that there were a few more such groups. This suggests that the Jaina women sometimes came together and engaged themselves in some kind of group activities.

Shrungarade of citation (15) identifies herself using the daughterly attribute of identity, but while most women use the term *putri* or *sutaa* for this purpose, she prefers the term *dharmaputri*. This term has not been explained either in the *Indian Epigraphical Glossary* of Sircar or in the Sanskrit Dictionary. (It could not be located in the *History of Dharma Shastra* of Kane either). However, the term *dharmaputra* has been explained in the above sources. The term conveys many meanings. According to Sircar[23] it means one theoretically accepted as a son. It also means[24] a lawful son, a son begotten from a sense of duty and not from mere lust or sensual pleasure, or any one regarded as son for the religious purpose, a spiritual son.

In all probability, the term *dharmaputri* must also have been used to indicate one of the above-mentioned meanings. To me, the connotation—one theoretically accepted as son (in this place daughter), seems most likely. It seems that Shrungarade was not the biological daughter of Pasa and his wife Valhade but was theoretically accepted as a daughter by them. Had she been the biological daughter, she could have simply used the term *putri*. Her giving the names of her foster parents at the cost of the names of her biological parents indicates that she held Pasa and Valhade in high esteem.

In the majority of group inscriptions, the donors were the members of patriarchal families. It has also been noted that majority the women donors of this period identified themselves by using their wifely attribute of identity. It seems therefore that the patriarchal families became stronger during this period and more and more women identified themselves with reference to their husbands' families. However, the epigraphic sources also show that some women also maintained good links with their natal families and made donations in association with their brothers and sisters. Probably many a time women went on pilgrimages along with their brothers and their families.

## Women renouncers

1. Samvat 1494, Paush, sudi 2, Sunday; by the order of Shri Jinasagarasuri, *gacchanayaka* of Khartara *gaccha*; *upadhyaya* Shri Vivekahansa, along with *pandita* Laxmisagara *gani*, Jayakirti *muni* Ratnalabha *muni*, Devasamudra *kshullaka* (junior monk), Dharmasamudra *kshullaka* and other monks, and *pravartini sadhvi* Bhavamati, Dharmaprabha *ganini*, Ratnasundari *sadhvi*, as well as San. Molha, San. Dungar, Shah Mela etc. *shravakas-shravikas* and the Vidhi *gaccha* community; always offer their salutations (*pranama*) to Shri Adinatha and Shri. Neminatha. (*APJLS*, 188, Abu)
2. --- Samavt 1603; the male disciples (*shishya*), Manikyacharitra, Gyanacharitra, Hemacharitra, Shivadhira, Dharmadhira; the female disciples (*shishyini*), *pravartini* Vidyasumati, Ratnasumati etc.; of Shri Palhanapuriya *gacchopadyaya* Shri. Vimalacharitra *gani*, _ with the advice of these renouncers, San. Hiraji, along with his family and the *sangha* completed the pilgrimage. Pa. Amarahansagani, Pa. Kanakasundara, Vimalacharana, Vijayvimala, Laxmidana, Vivekanandi, Laxmi *cula*. (*APJLS*, 214, Abu)
3. Samvat 1608, Vaishakha vadi 6, Friday, the disciples of Shri Kshamasagara --- of Vidhipaksha, Rishi Hira, --- *sadhvi* Nathi ---; Sa. Bhima, --- *shravika* Ladamade etc. along with the family, the whole *sangha* completed the pilgrimage of Abu successfully. (*APJLS*, 205, Abu)

4. *Rishi* Shri. *Pujya* Kshemasagara --- Vijamat's female disciple (*cheli*) ... samvat 1611, Paush vadi 5; *sadhvi* Suvira, *sadhvi* Bhana, Sa. Guna, Sa. Kheta --- (completed the pilgrimage successfully) (*APJLS*, 202, Abu)

In the available published Jaina epigraphic records, only four inscriptions of period II containing references to female renouncers could be spotted. This is rather strange in view of the fact that opting out of domestic life was open in theory to all Jaina women and a lot many women must have exercised the option. If so, it is difficult to figure out how are they missing as motivators of female donors. Against this background, four inscriptions making explicit mention of *sadhvis,* acquire an added importance by being rare. In citation (1) there is reference to Bhavamati *ganini,* Dharmaprabha *ganini* and Ratnasundari *sadhvi.* The inscription informs us that they formed part of the fourfold *sangha,* which visited Abu in 1494. They belonged to Khartaragaccha.

The *sadhvis* finding mention in (2) were a part of the family of disciples of monk Vimalacaritragani of Patanapuriyagaccha. They together motivated Haraji to take a pilgrimage to Abu in V.S. 1603. The names of these nuns were—*pravartini* Vidyasumati and *pravartini* Ratnasumati. At the end of this inscription a list of persons is given. It is not clear whether this list forms a part of the record or is a different record. This list gives us the name of Laxmichula. The term *chula* probably denotes a probationer who had not received *diksa.*[25] Citation (3) gives just one name, that of *sadhvi* Nathi. Citation (4) is also probably a list of pilgrims belonging to a religious group known as Vijamati. In this record two *sadhvis,* Suvira and Bhana find mention.

Significantly, all the four records come from Abu, which is located in Rajasthan near the border of Gujarat and none of them belong to Tapagaccha. It could therefore be that gender worked as a factor in the absence of women renouncers altogether from Satrunjaya and Girnar and only a rare presence in the epigraphic space of Abu—an equally sacred centre of Jainism.

Viewing the above facts in light of the following information we find:

Firstly, that the contemporary Tapagaccha nuns come mostly from Gujarat while those of Khartaragaccha are mostly from Rajasthan.[26] Secondly, in the *pattavalis* of Tapagaccha, we come across very few names of the *sadhvis*,[27] and thirdly, in the contemporary period nuns are generally not allowed to preach in Tapagaccha whereas in Anchalagaccha they are allowed to do so only if no monks are available. They are readily allowed to do so in the Khartaragaccha. Thus, it seems that within Murtipujakas, the Tapagaccha group is more conservative.[28]

It is quite possible that even during the period of the study Khartaragaccha monks and nuns were mostly concentrated in Rajasthan or north Gujarat and Tapagaccha monks and nuns in the rest of Gujarat and Saurashtra. Though the status of nuns was secondary to that of monks, gender discrimination may have been more in certain *gacchas* and less in others.

## Sati inscription

> Samvat 1672, Vaishakha sudi 3, Thursday; On this day Rupashri, Koma, Kesarajani, wives of San. Rupachanda, son of San. Sonapala, committed *sati*. During the reign of Badashah Salim Shri Jahangira, at Ahmedabad, on the bank of the river Sabarmati, they (the wives) became one with their husband (*samam bhavati*). Kuvarapala-Sonapala, sons of Rishabhdas of Osvala caste, *Vriddha shakha*, Lodha *gotra*. (*HIG-V*, 31)

After the death of Rupchanda, son of Sonapala and grandson of Rsabhadasa, his three wives Rupashri, Koma and Kesaranjani, committed *sati*.

There are positive indicators to show that the inscription belongs to a Jaina family—Rishabhadasa is a typical Jaina name. Secondly, Sonpala, Kuvarpala and Rupchanda take the attribute *sanghavi/sanghapati,* which is also a Jaina title. Thirdly, Osvala caste and Vriddha *shakha* are also found in some other Jaina inscription of the period. Lastly, according to Shastri,[29] two sons of the Rishabhadasa, Kuvarpala, and Sonpala, were very famous. They were ministers in the court of Jahangir and stayed at Agra. For sometime, they were also *diwans* of Gujarat. Rupchanda must have died when they were staying at Ahmedabad or while they halted at Ahmedabad on their way to Shatrunjaya for pilgrimage. As Shatrunjaya is a Jaina *tirtha*, the family of Rishabhadasa must have been a Jaina family.

This is indeed a rare record for the simple reason that self-immolation that is *sati* by Jaina widows is nowhere prescribed by Jaina scriptures. Therefore this *samagamana* or *sahagamana*, goes against the very philosophy of Jainism in which every individual—whether male or female—has to earn his/her own salvation by following the strict code of conduct so as to reach zero level *karma* status and achieve liberation from the round of births-deaths for ever. In all likelihood, the wives concerned or the family were under strong influence of Brahmanical practices. As mentioned above, the family members of these women were in the services of the Mughals and therefore probably came into close contact with the Rajputs. The women and/or their family members, it seems, were thus more influenced by the Rajput values than the religious prescriptions of their own religion.

## General pattern of women's inscriptions

A large majority of women of this period have identified themselves using wifely attribute of identity. Most of the inscriptions show a stereotypical pattern. Apart from the familial attributes, the other attributes of identify used by women were caste and the place to which they belonged. Some women used their religious attribute *shravika* or *sushravika*. Very rarely was the professional attribute (or the female versions of the professional attribute) such a as *sangavini* used.

Many women indicated the beneficiaries of their donations. The most frequently occurring beneficiaries were the donors themselves, followed by husband, mother/father or parents in-law.

In group donations, when women were the chief donors, they usually associated their sons, grandsons, sometimes daughters-in-law etc. In some cases they also associated their daughters, brothers and sisters, nephews, or in rare cases even their co-wives.

However, they never associated their husbands with them as donors.

The objects donated were the same as those appearing in the men's inscriptions. Overwhelming majority of the women donated small objects like images of *tirthankaras, chaturvinshatipattas* and the like. A few donated for the construction of small shrines or *devakulikas,* while only three women have contributed for the building of new temples or renovation of existing structures.

The most frequently occurring castes are Shrimala or Shrimali, Pragvata and Ukesh/Ush/Osvala. Some other castes, which find mention are Vayada, Disvala, Gurjar, Humbada and others.

## Comparison between the patterns of men's and women's inscriptions

During period II, most of the men identified themselves with reference to their parents. In the last chapter it had been noted that during period I, most men identified themselves with reference to their fathers alone and only some of them identified themselves with reference to both the parents. However, for period II, as stated above, most of the men identified themselves with reference to both of their parents. One reason for this could be that perhaps polygamy became more widespread and so it became necessary to indicate the mother's name. Nevertheless, it is also true that women as mothers were a source of identity to men. However, as is clear from the inscriptions, norms of identification were essentially patriarchal.

A vast majority of the women identified themselves using their wifely attribute of familial identity indicating the hold of patriarchy on them.

Thus, it could be said that both men and women were governed by the patriarchal value system while identifying themselves.

While choosing the beneficiaries of their donations, it can be seen that the proportion of men donating for the spiritual merit of their relatives is more than the proportion of women donating for the spiritual merit of their relatives. This observation is in keeping with the one made with the one made with regard to period I that the men were expected to provide material/financial support to fulfil the needs of their dependents. These needs also included the religious needs. It is this sense of duty, which guided men to donate for the spiritual merit of their relatives. Women on the other hand were not expected to support their family members financially and so many of them did not donate for the benefit of their family members. This observation stands for this period also.

However for period II there are a few more observations. Firstly, the proportion of women donating for their relatives is more than that during period I (though it is less than that for men). Secondly, we also note that the majority of the women who donated for the spiritual merit of their relatives, identified themselves using their wifely attribute of identity. It could be said, therefore, that as wives, some of them took upon themselves the responsibility of fulfilling the religious needs of their relatives, especially their spouses, and donated for their benefit.

In the group donations, norms of familial hierarchy were observed. When the chief donors were men, they usually associated their wives, sons, daughters-in-law etc. or their brothers, and sisters but did not associate the parents (citation (a) below). Similarly, when women were the chief donors, they usually associated their sons, sometimes along with daughters-in-law, grand sons etc. or their brothers and sisters or daughters, but did not associate their husbands (citation (b) below). There were also some group donations in which the chief donor was not indicated or because of the unclear phraseology, could not be identified (citation (c) below).

*Citation (a)*

Samvat 1516, Vaishakha shudi 3: Vimalanatha *panchatirthi*, dedicated for the merit of his father by Wagha, along with his wife Asi, their sons Goia, Balaraja, Amara and other family members; Wagha being the son (*suta*) of Man. Jesa and his wife Jasamade of Shri Shrimali caste --- (*JDLS-II*, 125, Vadodara)

*Citation (b)*

Samvat 1561, Jyeshtha shudi 2, Wednesday; an image of Shri Suvidhinatha, dedicated for the merit of self by Hansalade *sushravika*, along with her son San. Harsha, and other family members; Hansalade being the wife (*bharya*) of San. Hansaraja, son of San. Kuza and his wife Gurude of Shri Pragvata vansha, *Vriddha shakha* --- (*JDLS-II*, 691, Khambat)

*Citation (c)*

Samvat 1622, Magha vadi 2, Wednesday; a *siddhachakrapatta*, dedicated by soni Devachanda-soni Bhimaji, Bai Manai; --- (*JDLS-II*, 585, Khambat)

Objects donated by men and women were the same. The donations for building of a new temple or renovating the old ones were rare, both in men's as well as in women's inscriptions. However, the number of men making big donations was more than the number of women making big donations.

## Gender relations

Mother, as before, continued to be the most respected woman. We observe that mothers, along with fathers, formed a part of men's identity. Similarly, many a time, men chose their mothers (or parents) as the beneficiaries of their donations. On the other hand, in women's records, sons very rarely formed a part of women's identity. This is specially significant as K.K. Shah, in his study of the women's inscriptions of the ancient period, had noted that the Jaina women usually identified themselves by using their four fold familial status of being daughter, daughter-in-law, wife and mother.[30] As the beneficiaries of women donors also, sons appear very rarely. However, this does not mean that sons did not find mention in the women's records. Sons, as associate donors, found mention in the G-Woman inscriptions very frequently.

Jaina literary tradition accorded high status to mothers. Similarly, the Jaina law, by making wife the first heir to her husbands property, improved her position vis-à-vis her son.[31] The observations made in this research suggest that perhaps these ideals were also to a considerable extent put into practice by the Jainas of Gujarat.

The relationship between husband and wife was not of equality. Wife's subordination to her husband was taken for granted. Most of the women used their wifely attribute and saw themselves as the members of their husband's families. In the men's records, women as wives did not find mention when they were the sole donors except when the donation was made for the spiritual merit of wives. The familial hierarchy, which is observed in group donations, also suggests that wives were considered junior to their husbands. In G-Man inscriptions wives appear as associate donors and in G-Woman inscriptions husbands appear as the attribute of women's identity and not as associate donors. However, when women were the only daughters of their parents and thus were the heirs of their property, relationship between husband and wife was altered and in a few cases even reversed.

Presence of polygamy is attested by the sources, reducing women to the level of possessions.

The relationship between brothers and sisters seem to be of more equitable nature. The group-donations indicate this. Sometimes, in G-Woman inscriptions we find that the donor women associated their brothers. Similarly, in some G-Man inscriptions also we find sisters being associated as donors.

A woman was considered senior to the younger brothers of her husband. In a few G-Woman records we find women associating their younger brothers-in-law with them.

As far as the relationship between the parents and daughters was concerned, it seems they occupied less space in each other's familial world. The proportion of women using their daughterly attribute to identify themselves was very less. Parents were very rarely the beneficiaries when their daughters were the donors. Similarly, in the men's records also, only in a few cases we find the mention of daughters. In G-Man records only in rare cases, daughters were the associate donors.

The high percentage of group donations during this period indicates that at least on certain occasions men and women acted in association with each other. Family ties seem to have been strong.

On the whole, therefore, it could be said that the gender relations were guided by the patriarchal value system.

### To sum up

Group donations are a peculiar feature of the epigraphic records of this period. Members of these groups were usually the members of a patriarchal family. Perhaps, the patriarchal joint families became stronger during this period.

The manner in which men and women identified themselves, as also the manner in which they chose the beneficiaries of their donations, both indicate a considerable hold of patriarchy on them.

The women seem to have been indoctrinated to view themselves mainly as wives and the hold of patriarchy on them was quite complete. Nevertheless, they also kept contact with their natal families. It was expected of women that they keep the prestige of both the families by their conduct, i.e., their natal family and their family by marriage. In fact, the best way of eulogising a woman was to use the phrases such as *ubayakulanandadayini*, the one who gives happiness to both the families, etc.

The structure of most of the records is stereotypical. Most men and women use the set pattern to record their donations. However, some donors, both men and women, made a few variations in this pattern. These variations are indicative of the element of self-perception. They help us to spot those cases, which differed from the norms.

Relationship between husband and wife was not of equality. Wife's subordination to her husband was taken for granted and husbands held more power, financial or other, than their wives. However, in certain cases when wife was the only daughter of her father, the power-relationships were redefined and in some cases reversed. Even the relationship between the two families was altered. This is evident not only from the women's inscriptions, but also from men's inscriptions. For instance, there is an inscription by a man who calls his daughter a *putrika* and associates her in his donation.[32] In another case a man associates his daughter's son along with him.[33] In the record of Pahuti, she uses only her daughterly attribute of identity, but associates her husband in her donation.[34] A man Manika, donates for his maternal grandparents.[35]

In certain cases even when the women were not the only daughters and had brothers, they preferred to associate with their natal families as they derived their prestige from that family. Hirabai's inscription is one such record.[36]

It has been noted that women as mothers were a source of identity to men. In no other capacity could they provide identity to men. Nevertheless, in two cases this has happened. Hansa, a man calls himself husband of Sahajalde,[37] while Kalu calls himself *devara* or younger brother-in-law of Nathi.[38]

In group donations, generally the family members came together to donate, but in one case donation was made by a group of *shravikas*,[39] indicating the presence of a kind of women's association, which fulfilled their need of socialisation.

Jaina inscriptions of Gujarat are the main sources of this study. Therefore, it was natural to expect to find only Jainas as donors in the epigraphs. However, it seems that people of other faiths also sometimes made donations. The donor Devasiri calls herself daughter of *brahman* Sushharma. Nevertheless, it cannot be said whether she was a Jaina or non-Jaina or was married to a Jaina.

Jainas allowed women to opt out of the family life and pursue the career of a nun, but it also decreed that nuns were inferior to monks, and "a monk of three years standing may become the *upadhyaya* of a nun of sixty years".[40] Jainas of Gujarat seem to have followed this rule in letter and spirit. Only four records in which nuns find mention were found in the present collection of epigraphic records. The nuns have been accorded a negligible epigraphic space.

One epigraphic record, which goes totally against the Jaina Philosophy is the *sati* inscription cited above, which tells us that three wives of Rupcanda committed *sati*. Although this is a solitary record of its kind, it indicates cross-cultural influences and it is quite likely that a few more cases of *sati* might have taken place.

There are three inscriptions of this period in which women have donated for the construction or renovation of temples. This is especially significant as for period I, epigraphic record of the donation of a large sum by any woman was not noted. These three women were Indrabai, Tejalde and Hirabai. Thus, though women had less financial power than men did, on certain occasions they could control large sums of money.

Thus, more than four hundred inscriptions of women of this period throw light on various aspects of society like religion, customs, law etc., in relation to women.

## Notes

1. S.B. Raiyagor, *History of Gujarat* (New Delhi: S. Chand and Company, 1982), p. 334.
2. Ibid., pp. 234, 237.
3. C.B. Sheth, *Jainism in Gujarat* (Bombay: Shri Vijaydevsur Sangh Gyan Samiti, 1953), p. 199.
4. Ibid., pp. 203–4.
5. Ibid., p. 237.
6. Ibid., p. 261.
7. Ibid., pp. 270–71.
8. Motilal Mehata, *Jain Culture* (Varanasi: P.V. Research Institute, 1969), p. 42.
9. Hirabai Boradia, *Jaina Dharma Ki Pramukha Sadhviyam evam Mahilayan* (Varanasi: P.V. Research Institute, 1991), pp. 198–99.

10. H.G. Shastri, "The Early Jaina Epigraphs at Ahmedabad" in Hariyariya Rangarajan, G. Kamlakar and A.K.V.S. Reddy, (ed.), *Jainism: Art, Architecture, Literature and Philosophy* (Delhi: Sharada Publishing house, 2001), pp. 293–94.
11. See Chapter II, under the heading 'Women with daughterly attribute of identity'.
12. P.K. Gode and C.G. Karve, (ed.), *Prin. Vaman Shivaram Apte's: The Practical Sanskrit English Dictionary* (Poona: Prasad Prakashan, 1958), p. 856.
13. *Shat* pt. IV, p. 5, Inscription no. 10.
14. Hamchandracharya, *TSPC*, Vol. III, Tran, Helen M. Johnson (Baroda: Oriental Institute, 1949) p. 300. About the parents of Shantinatha, Hemachandra says—"Sometime passed for king Vishvasena and queen Achira absorbed in the pleasure of sovereignty rejoicing like Indra and Indrani."
15. Nalini Joshi, *Jaina Agamat Stri*, (Pune: K.K. Jain, 2000), p. 46.
16. See Chapter II, Citation no. 12 under the heading "Women with wifely attribute of identity".
17. See Chapter II, under the heading ' Women with daughterly attribute of identity'.
18. Men and women generally used only the short forms to indicate their professional attributes. For instance, Sa. indicated Sahu and San. indicated *Sanghavi*. There are one or two records where women have used the full forms of their professional attributes. These are the feminine forms of the men's professional attributes. Therefore it could be assumed that wherever the short forms of professional attributes are used by women they stand for the feminine forms of men's attributes.
19. *JPLS*, p. 6.
20. *APJLS,* p. 17.
21. C.B. Sheth, op. cit., pp. 222–23.
22. *APJLS,* pp. 162–63. Inscription nos. 408, 410 and 411.
23. D.C. Sircar, *Indian Epigraphical Glossary* (Delhi: Motilal Banarasidas, 1966), p. 94
24. P.K. Gode and C.G. Karve, op. cit., p. 856.
25. N. Shanta, *The Unknown Pilgrims* (Delhi: Shri Satguru Publications, 1997) p. 187.

26. N. Shanta, op. cit., pp. 435–36.
27. Hirabai Boradia, op. cit., p. 197.
28. Nalini Balbir, "Women and Jainism in India", *Women in Indian Religions*, (ed.), Arvind Sharma (New Delhi: Oxford Univ. Press, 2002) pp. 90–91.
29. HIG-V, p. 55.
30. K.K. Shah, *The Problem of Identity: Women in Early Indian Inscriptions* (New Delhi: Oxford University Press, 2001) p. 113.
31. C.R. Jain, *The Jain Law,* (Madras: The Devendra Printing & Publishing Co. Ltd., 1926), p. 77.
32. See Citation no. 9, under the heading 'Men's inscriptions'.
33. See Citation no. 2, under the heading 'Men's inscriptions'.
34. See explanation for Citation no. 17, under the heading 'G-Woman inscriptions'.
35. See explanation for Citation no. 17, under the heading 'G-Woman inscriptions'. (JDLS-II, p. 203).
36. See Citation no. 27, under the heading 'G-Woman inscriptions'.
37. See Citation no. 1 under the heading 'Men's inscriptions'.
38. See Citation no. 7 under the heading 'Men's inscriptions'.
39. See Citation no. 25 under the heading 'G-Woman inscriptions'.
40. S.B. Deo, History of Jain Monachism, *Bulletin of the Deccan College. Research Institute,* (June 1954–March 1955), p. 467.

# 4

# Women with Familial and Non-Familial Attributes of Identity

## 18th and 19th Centuries C.E. (Period III)

During the 18th century Gujarat faced political instability, which in turn created social and economic insecurity. The mental horizon of the people was shrinking. People lived under all sorts of superstitions. Inhuman customs like *sati* and female infanticide prevailed in some parts of Gujarat. Moreover, the social set-up did not allow the scope for new changes, though some of the saint poets like Akha and Bhoja Bhagat articulated some of the social evils.[1]

The establishment of the British rule in Gujarat gradually transformed the administrative and legal structure. Transport and communication developed and the industrialisation started taking place. The British also brought about some economic and social changes. Because of these reasons, the mental horizon of the people started gradually expanding once again. A new middle class, the product of all these factors, realised the importance of new education, which created a climate for new social and cultural outlook. As a result, the new intelligentsia started examining the social and religious relationship with a critical eye.[2]

With the initiative of the English educated elite, social and religious reform movements saw the light of the day. Although in a society as complex as India, reform movement was not a new phenomenon. However, with the establishment of the British rule, Indian society was confronted with an entirely different kind of heterogenetic cultural tradition. The features like liberalism, individualism and experimental attitude marked this tradition.[3]

Most of the socio-religious reform movements were aimed at women; they addressed the issues such as maltreatment of widows, child marriage, ban on widow remarriage, custom of *sati*, polygamy and so on. Many new organisations were established for bringing about such reforms. Durgaram Mehtaji (1809–76), a Nagar *brahman*, who is known as the father of modern reform movement in Gujarat, started 'Manav Dharma Sabha' in Surat in 1844. In approach it was similar to Brahmo Samaj. Ranchhodadas Girdharbhai—father of new education in Gujarat was the first president of 'Gnan Prakash Mandali', while Kavi Narmad started 'Buddivardḩaka Sabha' in 1851. These organisations and their monthly organs as well as newspapers, influenced the social life of Gujarat. However, they did not aim at restructuring the society at large. They wanted to infuse into the existing social structure new ways of life and thought.[4]

A.K. Forbes started Gujarat Vernacular Society (GVS) in 1848 at Ahmedabad. Its main objective was the development of Gujarati language and literature. It also became a vehicle for propagating new ideas conducive to social change in Gujarat. GVS took charge of 'Buddhi Prakash' from April 1854, which was originally started by 'Buddhi Prakash Mandali' in 1850.[5] GVS advocated women's education and established the first school for girls in 1850 with the generous donation from *shetani* Harkunvar, a rich enlightened widow,[6] who was a Jaina woman.

The first phase of reform movement, which began in 1844, was more or less over by the end of seventies of the 19th century. The second phase started after 1880s. The reformers of the first phase were criticised by those of the second phase, who were conservative in approach. The conservatives were not against modern cultural trends; their main crusade was against grafting of the western cultural tradition on the Indian society.[7] Govardhanram Tripathi, through the medium of literature, (author of '*Saraswatichandra*') placed the controversy pertaining to tradition and modernity in the right perspective and evolved a new cultural synthesis.[8]

The Hindus as well as the Jainas were involved in these reform movements. In fact, among the wealthy people who supported the reform movements by their generous donations, there were many Jaina merchants also.

The reformist changes of the 19th century transformed into progressive continuity in the early decades of the 20th century.[9] These socio-religious movements may not have shown immediate results, but they certainly brought about a change in the mindset of the people, both Hindu as well as Jaina.

This is, in brief, the outline of the social history of Gujarat of 18th and 19th centuries. It will serve as a background for the study of the Jaina inscriptions of this period, which is undertaken in this chapter.

The total number of inscriptions belonging to this period is more than 250. Out of these, women's inscriptions are 56 (21%). This percentage is higher than for period I as well as period II. However, the percentage of women donors is the highest for the 18th century (24%), whereas the same for 19th century is 19 per cent.

Strange as it might seem, a period of political instability and socio-economic insecurity is also marked by the increasing visibility of women in the public sphere appropriating epigraphic space. This reflects clearly on the one hand that the periods of peace and stability strengthens the hold of patriarchy, and on the other hand, that periodisation in available historiography needs modification when women's experience is also taken into account. The high visibility of women, in other words, during a period of socio-political turmoil cannot be taken as mere coincidence.

Another important observation about the epigraphs of this period is that the percentage of group donations is much less (app. 10%), than the same for period II (app. 50%).

For the analysis of inscriptions in this chapter the same pattern, which was followed in the previous two chapters, has been followed.

Since most of the inscriptions of this period do not contain the clause indicating the beneficiary of donation, the scope for inquiry is limited by that factor.

## Pattern of men's inscriptions

A large number of inscriptions of this period are very brief. The familial attributes of identity used by men are the name of the father, lineage, parents, grandparents etc., but many men have not mentioned their familial attributes at all. The other attributes of identity used by men are caste, place name, religious affiliation and profession. Some use caste name and personal name, while others use place name and personal name, while still others use all the attributes together. Thus, it can be said that men used the various combinations of the above mentioned attributes while constructing their identity.

Donation was made for one or more of the following purposes, as was the case in the previous centuries:

1. Building of new temples, *dharmashalas* etc.
2. Undertaking the repair work of the existing structures
3. *devakulikas* or small shrines
4. Images of *tirthankaras*
5. Images of the monks or their foot impressions
6. Images of *shravaka*, *shravikas*
7. *samavasarana*
8. *siddhachakra*

Donations for building temples and *dharmashalas* or for undertaking repair works must have been a costly affair and therefore such donations were very rare. The smaller objects, which required less amount of money such as the images of *tirthankaras*, *siddhachakara* and the like, were, as in the previous periods, the most common objects of donation. Donating for *devakulikas* was rarer than the images. This was the general pattern of men's records.

One record, which is the longest record of the period under review, belongs to the descendants of Shantidasa, the Jaina magnate and the first *nagrashetha* of Ahmedabad.[10] It contains names and descriptions of the religious activities of its members, which include women as well. It throws some light on the gender relations. As the references to women are scattered here and there in the inscription, it is not possible to cite them all. However, before taking up the analysis of women's inscriptions it will be pertinent to describe the contents of this inscription.

### Hemabhai's inscription at Shatrunjaya[11]

Shantidasa Jawahari flourished during the reign of Jahangir and Shah Jahan. His great resources as financer and business connections as a jeweller enabled him to enjoy considerable favour and influence at the imperial court at Delhi. He was the first *nagrashetha* of Ahmedabad by popular voice, and this title, with its attached status and conventional functions, was handed down in his family until recent times.[12] In 1725, a grandson of *shetha* Shantidasa named *shetha* Khushalcanda, saved Ahmedabad from being ransacked by the Marathas. With his own money and at the risk of his life, he bought off the invaders.[13] Hemabhai, whose inscription is being referred to in this place, was the grandson of Khushalcanda.

The family background of Hemabhai has been given to have an idea about the power and prestige, which the family commanded.

The record starts with the veneration to Gautamnatha and states that Kuvarpala Ayaraja took the vow of *shravakadharma*, that is he became a Jaina householder. He belonged to Osvala caste and was a resident of Ahmedabad. Then a long list of his descendants is given. In Rajnagar, on Shantidasa was first conferred the title of *shetha*. The family tree of Shantidasa is as follows:

**(1) Family tree of Shantidasa**

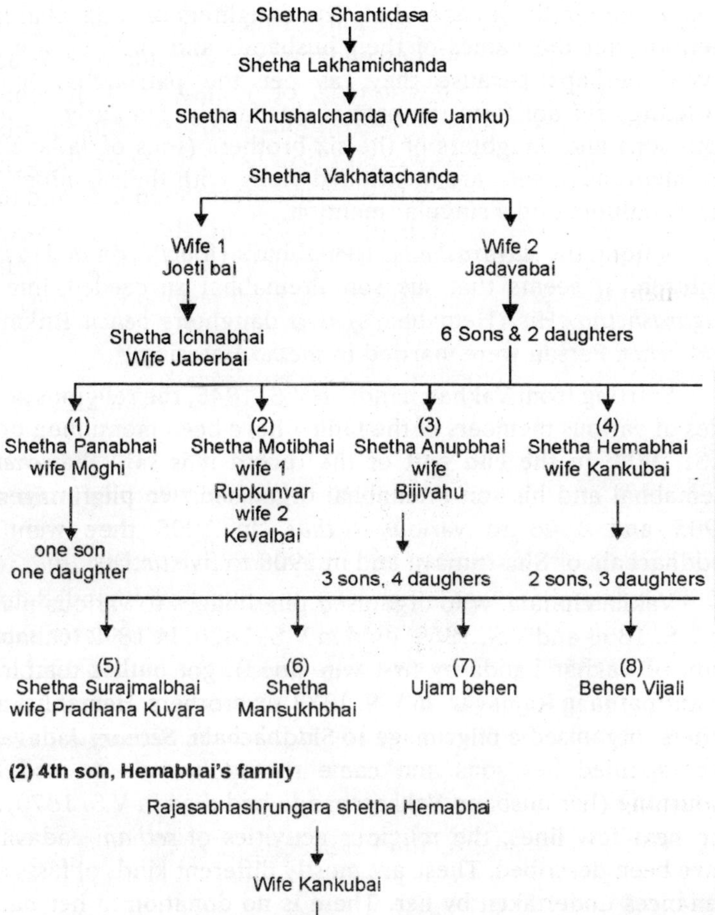


**(2) 4th son, Hemabhai's family**

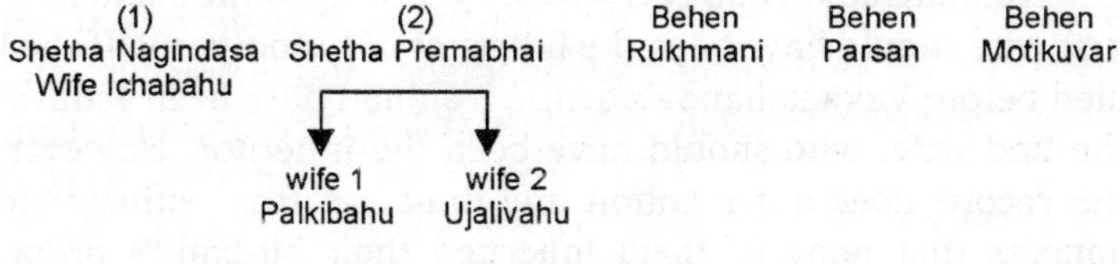

Vakhatchanda had two wives. First was Joetibai and second was Jadavabai. Mainly, the record describes the religious activities of the family of Jadavabai. The daughters of Jadavabai find mention but the names of their husbands and children are not given, perhaps because they, as per the patriarchal family structure, did not form the part of this family. Similarly, though both sons and daughters of the six brothers (sons of Jadavabai) are mentioned, sons are mentioned along with their families but the daughters find a singular mention.

Among the *nagarashetha* Hemabhai's (fourth son of Jadava) children, it seems that his son Premabhai succeeded him as *nagarashetha*. His (Hemabhai's) two daughters *behen* Rukmani and *behen* Parsan were married to *shetha* Hatesing.[14]

Starting from Vakhatchanda in V.S. 1845, the religious activities of various members of the family have been mentioned up to V.S. 1904. In the end part of the record it is said that *shetha* Hemabhai and his son Premabhai organised two pilgrimages in 1905 and 1908 to various *tirthas*. In 1905 they went to Siddhachala or Shatrunjaya and in 1908 to five *tirthas*.

Vakhatchanda, who organised pilgrimages to various places in V.S. 1868 and V.S. 1869, died in V.S. 1870. In 1872 Ichhabhai (son of Vakhatchanda by first wife Joeti), got built a temple of Shantinatha in Rajnagar. In V.S. 1873 six brothers, Hemabhai and others, organised a pilgrimage to Siddhachala. *Sethani* Jadavabai accompanied her sons and came to Siddhachala to end her mourning (her husband Vakhatchanda had died in V.S. 1870). In the next few lines, the religious activities of *sethani* Jadavabai have been described. These are mostly different kinds of fasts and penances undertaken by her. There is no donation in her name. She breathed her last on Siddhachala in V.S. 1882.

Vakhatchanda had two wives. According to the Jaina law, his first wife should have been the inheritor of his property. If she had died before Vakhatchanda's death, it should have been Jadavabai, the 2nd wife, who should have been the inheritor. However, as the record does not mention any donation from either wife, it appears that none of them inherited their husband's property. Hemabhai, the fourth son succeeded Vakhatchanda as *nagarashetha*. He, or his eldest brother, or all of them, may have inherited the property. It seems that in certain cases where the sons were influential, the inheritance rights of mothers were overruled. The women in whose name some donations have been made are—Ujamben, Ujali, Ben Phuli, Sardar Kuwar Kankubai, and Prasanna. Ujamben got constructed one *dharmashala* in Rajnagar and got repaired the new temple of Mahavirasvami. She also finds mention as a donor in two more records, the details of which have been given under the head 'women with daughterly attribute of identity'.

Apart from the above record of Hemabhai, abstracts of a few more records of donations by the members of this family are also available.[15] There are eleven records, out of which the majority are by the women of the family. Two women who have given big donations are Icchavahu, wife of Nagindas, and Phulkuvara, daughter of Anoopbhai. The point worth noting about these inscriptions is that the daughters of the family identify themselves as the daughters, while the wives identify themselves by using their wifely attribute. This indicates quite clearly that the women in general and women of this family in particular, chose that attribute of identity, which added to their prestige. In identifying themselves their agency is quite clear.

Hemabhai's inscription is an example of a patriarchal joint family. It consists of a senior couple, their sons, daughters, daughters-in-law, grandsons, granddaughters-in-law, and so on. The daughters and sisters of the family find mention, but not their husbands and children. Sons-in-law and their children strictly belonged to other families. Not only in this record, but also in all the records considered for this research, there is no inscription in which son-in-law finds mention though there is atleast one records where the donor identifies himself as the son-in-law. Polygamy was fairly common. Some men of this family had two or three wives but mothers finds a respectable mention.

From Hemabhi's record and the other records of the family, it can be said that the women did get some epigraphic space and that they made use of this space in such a way so as to enhance their prestige.

## Women's inscriptions

In this chapter, for the purpose of analysis, women's inscriptions have been classified under the following heads:

1. Women with wifely attribute of identity,
2. Women with daughterly attribute of identity,
3. Women with motherly attribute of identity,
4. Women without any familial attribute, and
5. Women renouncers.

## Women with wifely attribute of identity

Below are cited a few inscriptions in which women use their wifely attribute to identify themselves. Citations (6) and (8) are long and therefore only relevant portions of these records have been cited. Some portion of citation (4) is mutilated, as per the source book.

1. Samvat 1761, Vaishakha shudi 5, Thursday; a Shantinatha *panchatirthi*, dedicated from her own resources (*swadrawyena*) by Jivana, wife (*bharya*) of Dharmana, son of Samrutha of Shrimali caste, *Vriddha shakha*, inhabitant of Shri Radhanpur --- (*RPLS*, 384, Radhanpur)
2. Samvat 1828, Phalguna shudi 2, Friday; an image of Vira dedicated for the merit of her father by Dhana, wife (*bharya*) of Khubachanda, son of Maniyara Rishabh --- (*RPLS*, 436, Radhanpur)
3. Samvat 1836, Shaka Samvat 727 (sic), Magha, Krishna *paksha* 7, Thursday; an image of Shri Adinatha, dedicated by Rupabai, sister-in-law (*bhojai*) of *mantri* Ghudasia Kapura Hiradasa of Hucchamaccha caste, *Vriddha shakha* --- (*JDLS-I*, 436, Idar)
4. Samvat 1893, Maha sud 1, Wednesday; an image of Shri Vasupujya, dedicated by Khemi, wife (*bharika*) of Kaniyana Meghaji of Shrimali caste --- (*RPLS*, 457, Radhanpur)
5. Samvat 1898, Phagua shudi 7, Saturday; an image of Shri Sumatinatha, dedicated at the advice (*upadesha*) of Shri

Jayakirtisuri of Shri Anchala *gaccha*, for the merit of self by Hirade and Malahanade, wives of Devasi, son of Vya. Sunta and his wife Suhaba of Shri Shrimali caste --- (*JDLS-I*, 1034, Ahmedabad)

6. In Ahmedabad, during the reign of East India Company, lived Sha. Shri Nihalachand of Osvala caste. Sheth Hatesingh was the descendant of this Sha. Nihalachand and the son of Kesarisingh and his wife Suraja. Hatesingh earned ample wealth and also donated it freely. He had two wives (*bharya*), Rukmini, and the wise Harkuvara and a son by name Jayasingh. After the death of Hatesingh, in accordance with his wishes, Harkuvara got completed the construction of the temple which was started by Hatesingh. She also performed the consecration celebrations etc. On this occasion many people from far and nearby places were invited. Many monks and the *sanghapatis* had come along with the *sangha*. In all nearly four lakh people attended the function. In spite of being a woman, she handled such complex tasks, which even a man could not have done. The consecration ceremony started on Samvat 1903, Shaka 1768, Magha shudi 6, and continued for almost twenty days. --- (*PJLS*, 556 Ahmedabad)

7. Samvat 1907, Vaishakha vadi 11; --- an image of Shri Vasupujya dedicated by Bai Rangu, wife (*bharya*) of Sa. Tarachanda, son of Sa. Ichachanda, of Shri Shrimali caste, Laghu *shakha* --- (*Shat* 585, Shatrunjaya)

8. --- Samvat 1916, Vaishakh, krishna 6, Thursday; a temple (*Shrivasupujyaprasada*) built, and various benefactions made by Bai Shiva, the second wife of Shri. Karamachanda, son of *parekha* Mithubhai and his wife Benakumavra, --- of Nema caste, *Vriddha shakha*, inhabitants of Kapadavanaja in Gujarat, the first wife of Karamachand being *ubhayakulavanti* bai Jadava --- (*Shat*, 153, Shatrunjaya)

9. Samvat 1920, Pha. va.2; an image of Mallinathaji dedicated by Mahatabakumara, wife (*bharya*) of Sa. Pratapsinghji. (*APJLS*, 18, Abu)

10. Samvat 1929, Va. Mahasudi 7, Thursday; an image of Shri Munisuvratajina, dedicated for her soul (*swa-atmarthe*) by Khushali, wife (*bharya*) of Doshi Dalchachanda Mayachanda --- (*RPLS*, 473, Radhanpur)

The term used for indicating wifely status, in most of the records is *bharya*. Shemi of citation (4) however prefers the term *bharika*. Jivana of citation (1) has donated *Shantinatha panchatirthi*. Her record is brief but she has not forgotten to mention that she is donating from her own money (*swadravyena*). Such words and phrases are very important as they may give us some idea about the financial capability and power of the donor woman. In the present collection of inscriptions, this is the only record by a woman where this term has been used. Therefore, it seems quite likely that many women received money from their male relatives for donating. Jivana is trying to indicate that she did not receive any such money but donated from her own resources. Considering the decontextualised nature of the record, it is very difficult to say anything about Jivana's source of income. Maybe she had sufficient *stridhana*, or else had inherited her husband's or father's property. The possibility that she herself was engaged in some kind of business or profession is less likely, but cannot be ruled out altogether.

Dhana of citation (2) donated for the spiritual merit of her father. Very few donors of this period have mentioned the beneficiary of their donation.

The donors of citations (5), (6), (8) and (9) were from a polygamous marriage. In (5), (6) and (8) the phraseology clearly indicates the polygamous nature of marriage. In (9) it has to be inferred. In this record, the donor is Mehataba. She used the suffix *kumar* which probably indicates that she was the second wife. In citation (6) two wives of Devasi, Hirade and Malhanade are the donors. The two co-wives probably maintained cordial relations. Such records have been noted for period I and period II as well. The women in patriarchal societies were expected to maintain hearty relations with their co-wives. The women in such records seem to be fulfilling this expectation. Shiva of (8) tells us that she is the second wife of Karmachand. She not only gives the name of her co-wife but also attaches the attribute *ubhayakulvanti*, the one who glorified both the families by her conduct, to her name. Shiva is one of the very few women who has contributed for the building of a temple. The record also tells us that she spent money on various other religious activities.

According to the abstract of this record (8), given in *E.I.*, Vol. II (p. 85), the donation was made by the family of Sa Hiraji, an ancestor of Bai Shiva's husband Karmachand. However, this reading of the record does not seem to be correct. In the above source, the author has taken Shivena to be the name of Karmachand's wife, but the correct name seems to be just Shiva. What seems appropriate is that in the record, according to Sanskrit grammar, third or the instrumental case of Shiva, that is Shivena, meaning 'by Shiva' is used. This indicates that Shiva is indeed the donor. Though being a feminine name, the masculine case has been used here, but such mistakes do occur at times in the epigraphic records.

Inscription (6) is yet another important record. It describes the various religious activities of Harkumari, second wife of *shetha* Hatisingh of Ahmedabad. Hatisingh had earned ample money on his own merit. He started the work of constructing a temple, but he left for his heavenly journey before this work could be completed. According to his wishes his virtuous wife Harkumarika completed the work. This has been described as the most famous and most beautiful of the Jaina temples of Ahmedabad, built in modern times by Commissariat in his book *A History of Gujarat*. With great pomp and show, she celebrated the consecration and other ceremonies in V.S. 1903. The inscription says that she invited people from far and near by places. Four lakh people participated in the celebrations that continued for some days. It has been said of her that, although she is a woman, she has done that work which even a man would not be able to do. This statement is very important to have a peep into the concepts of masculine and feminine. According to the gender norms of Indian society of the period, it was believed that men were capable of undertaking greater responsibilities outside home. It was men who could accomplish huge and complex tasks. On the other hand, it was thought that women did not have the capacity to undertake such tasks, especially outside home. However, Harkumarika successfully handled the activities of completing the construction and organising consecration ceremonies. This record of Harkunvar *shethani* is similar to Tejalde's record, which is cited in the previous chapter. Both Tejalde and Harkunvar carried out the wishes of their respective husbands. The phrase used in Tejalde's record is *Tejapala pradattadnyaya,*[16] whereas that used in Harkunvara's record is *bhartruvakyaihikriya sarvo*. A good and virtuous wife was expected not only to be obedient to her husband, but also to merge her identity with that of her husband. Both these records stress this quality of the donor women.

The two records are similar in yet another way. They show that sometimes Jaina women became empowered after the death of their husbands. Jaina law gives widows the right to inherit their husband's property. The records like these show that law was also practiced. However, it was the eldest wife who inherited the husbands property,[17] and Harkunvar was the second wife. So how could she inherit the property then? Luckily, there is some information about Harkunvar from the literary sources. These literary sources throw more light on Harkunvar's life. Harkunvar was popularly known as Harkor *shethani*. She was the enlightened widow of Hatesingh Kesarsingh, a rich merchant of Ahmedabad. He was nearly twenty-four years older than she was and was married twice before marrying Harkunvar. His first wife Rukmini had become blind and was barren, so he married Prasanna. The two were daughters of Hemabhai, the descendent of Shantidasa. Prasanna died without bearing him a child. Harkunvar was his third wife. Thus, it seems that as Harkunvar's elder co-wife was blind, therefore Harkunvar either inherited or controlled her husband's property. Kunjalata Shah writes in her paper that Harikunvar also did not bear any child.[18] But, the inscription tells us that Hatesingh had a son named Jaisingh. Harkunvar was only twenty-six years old when Hatesingh died in 1846. At that time, social reform had just begun in Gujarat. Harkunvar was influenced by the progressive thoughts of the day, and involved herself in the reformist activities. She did not confine her donative activities to the religious purposes alone but also spent her money generously for social purposes. In 1850 C.E., Harkor started a girls' school in the city for the first time. Harkor had empathy towards miseries and deprivations of widows. She took up the cause of widows' education and admitted them to her school. She also donated for the provincial college. She, along with her elder co-wife Rukmini, gave a huge donation of fifty-two thousand rupees towards hospitals in the city. These are only a few of Harkunvar's acts of benevolence.[19]

This inscription of Harkunvar, being religious in nature, throws light only on the religious acts of Harkunvar. The year of Harkunvar's record is V.S. 1903, that is 1846 C.E., probably just a few days after her husband's death. Most of her donations for social purposes were made after 1950 C.E. Therefore, it is quite natural that these do not find mention in her inscription. The literary sources tell us about her other activities and provides a social background to the record.

The donor Rupabai of citation (3) identifies herself not as wife but as a sister-in-law. Yet her record has been included under the heading 'women with wifely attribute of identity', as this familial attribute of hers relates to her husband's family. She does not give the name of her husband but gives the name of her brother-in-law. Probably her brother-in-law was an influential person. It is also likely that she was widowed early in life and was living under his protection. In any case, in absence of any other information, it is very difficult to figure out the exact reason for this.

Bai Khusali of citation (10) has stated the purpose of her donation as *swa-atmarthe*, i.e., for the purpose of one's soul. This reflects awareness of the Jaina doctrine, according to which every individual, whether a man or a woman, has to strive for the liberation of one's soul from the rounds of births and deaths. This has to be done by following the strict code of conduct. As against this, the *sati* inscription mentioned in the previous chapter[20] shows the ignorance of either the women concerned or their family, about the Jaina doctrine. Thus, it can be said that the level of awareness about the Jaina doctrines was not the same in case of all Jaina women. Some women were better informed about these while others were less so, or perhaps they were more influenced by the social norms.

Citation (7) of Bai Rangu, is an example of a stereotypical record. Here Rangu has used the set pattern to record her donation without making any change in it.

**Women with daughterly attribute of identity**

1. Samvat 1853, Ashadha shudi 10, Thursday; dedicated by Lakhmi, daughter (*putri*) of Sa. Sarupachanda of Shrimali caste. (*Shat*, 392, Shatrunjaya)
2. Samvat 1892, Vaishakha shudi 3, Friday; a small shrine (*deri*) and images of Shri Parshvanatha, Shri Shantinatha, dedicated by Bai Aval, daughter (*dikari*) of Doshi. Abhechanda, inhabitant of Bhavanagara, belonging to Tapa *gaccha* --- (*Shat*, 568, Shatrunjaya)
3. Samvat 1893, Magha shudi 10, Wednesday; an image of Shri Suvidhinathajina, dedicated by Manchi, daughter (*putri*) of Sa. Bhushanadasa of Osvala caste, *Vriddha shakha*, inhabitant of Rajanagara --- (*JDLS-I*, 403, Manasa)
4. Samvat 1893, Magha shudi 10, Wednesday; an image of Shri Kunthunatha dedicated by Sankali, daughter (*putri*) of Sa. Bhushanadasa of Osvala caste, ... inhabitant of Rajanagara --- (*JDLS-I*, 409, Manasa)
5. Samvat 1912, Magha krishna 5, Thursday, an image of Dharmanatha, dedicated by Bai Dosi, daughter (*putri*) of ... son of ... of Visashrimali caste, inhabitant of Rajanagara --- (*RPLS*, 465, Radhanpur)
6. Samvat 1912, Kartika vadi 5, Wednesday; an image of Shri Ajitanatha, dedicated by Bai Benkuvara, daughter (*putri*) of Do. Harkhaji Hiraji of Visanema caste, inhabitant of Surat --- (*Shat*, 493, Shatrunjaya)

7. Samvat 1921, Shaka 1786, Magha sudi 7, Thursday; an image of Shri Shantinathaji, dedicated for the merit of self by Ben Ujamaba daughter (*putri*) of *shetha* Vakhatachanda and his wife Jadavabai; Vakhatachanda being the son of --- of Osvala *visha* caste, *Vriddha shakha* --- (*Shat*, 473, Shatrunjaya)

Very few women of this period prefer to identify themselves using the daughterly attribute of identity. There are only seven such inscriptions, which is nearly thirteen per cent of the total women's inscriptions of period III. All these records have been cited. Only two of these seven women have identified themselves with reference to both the parents. The rest have done so with reference to their fathers alone, indicating the hold of patriarchal values on them. The records are brief and give us no idea about the marital status of these women. Apart from their daughterly attribute, most of them have given the name of the caste to which they belonged. A few of them have also indicated the place where they hailed from. Most of them have given their religious affiliation, but strangely enough, none of them has used the religious attribute *shravika*.

Most of the records are in Sanskrit or Sanskrit mixed with Gujarati. However, a few are in Gujarati alone. Citation (2) is one such record. The donor of this record, Bai Aval has contributed for the construction of *dehari* or a small shrine. Donors of citations (3) and (4) seem to be sisters. They are the daughters of Bhushanadasa. Ujamba of citation (7) was the descendant of Shantidasa, of Ahmedabad. She donated the image of Shantinatha. This epigraph of Ujambai is located at Ujambai *tunk*. This *tunk* is named after her as she got it built.[21] Ujambai also finds mention in a few more inscriptions. In the inscription of Hemabhai,[22] her brother, she finds mention as the one who got a *dharmashala* built. In another record, which is located at her own *tunk*, she finds mention as one of the donors of the image.

Samvat 1893, Shaka 1658 (sic), Magha, sukla paksha,10 Wednesday; an image of Shri Mahavirasvami, dedicated, in the name of and for the merit of Jadavabai, wife of Se.

> Khushalachanda, son of ---; by *shetha* Hemabhai along with ... *shetha* Manasukhabhai, *ben* Ujamabai and other family members --- (*Shat*,169, Shatrunjaya)

In yet another record also Ujamba finds mention as one of the donors. The donation is by Ujamba's family (Shat, 494).

In none of the above mentioned records of Ujamba, we find mention of her husband or children. The possibilities are that either she was married but was widowed early in life and so had no family of her own, or she was not married at all, or else she was married but preferred to identify herself as a daughter because her natal family was exceptionally rich and influential. In any case, finances must not have been a problem for her. The amounts she must have received as gifts from her father and brothers must have been sufficient for her to make all those donations. The Jaina law also gives certain share to unmarried sisters.[23] She might possibly have received a certain share if she was unmarried. As noted before, like Ujambai, other daughters of the family have also identified themselves by giving their daughterly attribute. It is unlikely that all of them were unmarried or widowed. Their using the daughterly attribute only highlights the importance attached by these women to their connection with their natal family.

The other records under this head follow a conventional pattern.

### Women with motherly attribute of identity

> Samvat 1893, Shaka 1758, Magha Shukla paksha 10, Wednesday; an image of Parshvanatha, dedicated for the merit of their husband and their son by Ajab and Manakuvara, first and the second mothers (*mata*) of Sa. Pitamara, son of Sa. Sakalachanda, son of --- of Shrimali caste, *Laghu shakha*, inhabitant of Ahmedabad --- (*Shat*, 420, Shatrunjaya)

This is the only inscription of this period where two women use their motherly status as the familial attribute of their identity. The relevant portion of this record has been cited. The inscription says that Bai Ajab and Mankunvar, first and the second mothers of

Pitamara, donated the image of Parshvanatha for the spiritual merit of their husband and their son. In the present collection of inscriptions, we do find women identifying themselves as first and the second wives of someone. However, this particular record is the only one where the women identify themselves as first and the second mothers. From the record we do not even come to know who is the biological mother of Pitamar. It seems that Bai Ajab and Mankunvar were not just trying to exhibit cordial relations but probably that the relations between these women were really warm. They also give the name of their husband, but only as the mark of their son's identity, not as the attribute of their identity. The possibilities are—firstly, the husband was already dead and they were dependent on their son, and secondly, the husband was alive but retired from the business, which was now managed by the son. The possibility that both of them are either dead or alive also exists. It could be that loss of both had brought them emotionally together.

This is yet another record in which co-wives exhibit cordial relations. The society appreciated such behaviour as that befitting ideal wives.

### Women using only personal names as attribute of identity

Eleven inscriptions in which women figure without their familial attributes have been cited.

1. Samvat 1758, Shaka 1623, Kartika sudi 2, Wednesday; the foot impressions (*paduka*) of Bhattraka Shri. 5 Buddhisagarasurishwara, dedicated for the merit by *sushravika* Rahivâbai, at the request of Sha. Somachanda, Sha. Hirachanda, inhabitants of Shri. Rajanagara --- (*Shat* 148, Shatrunjaya)
2. Samvat 1769, Vaishakha vadi 1, Thursday; an image of Shri Shantinatha, dedicated by Bai Gangai and Bai Kasavi, of Shrimali caste, *Vriddha shakha*, inhabitants of Radhanpura --- (*RPLS*, 394, Radhanapur)

3. Samvat 1769, Posh vadi 1, Thursday; an image of Shri Shantinatha, dedicated by Bai Jayavanta, inhabitant of Radhanpur --- (*RPLS*, 388, Radhanpur)
4. Samvat 1824, Shaka 1689, mahasudi 10, Thursday; a *siddhachakra* dedicated for charity (*paropakarartham)* by *shravika* Telabai, inhabitant of Bahanapura --- (*JDLS-I*, 125, Chanasma)
5. Samvat 1828, Chaitra vadi 13, a *siddhachakra*, dedicated by *shravika* Valibai --- (*Shat*, 396, Shatrunjaya)
6. Samvat 1837, Ashwina sudi 13, a *siddhachakra*, dedicated by *shravika* Jelabai --- (*Shat*, 380, Shatrunjaya)
7. Samvat 1838, Vaishakha vadi 2; a *siddhachakra*, dedicated by *shravika* Acharata of Shrimali caste --- (*Shat*, 395, Shatrunjaya)
8. Samvat 1839, Vaishakha shudi 6, Wednesday; an image of Shri Vasupujya dedicated for the merit of self, on the occasion of completing the *Rohini tapa* (a kind of penance), by the community of *shravikas* of Shri Darbhati --- (*JDLS-I*, 12, Dabhoi)
9. Samvat 1848, Kartika vadi 6, dedicated (an image) by Rupa *shravika* of Vijaya *gaccha*. (*RPLS*, 447, Radhanpur)
10. Samvat 1893, Mahasudi 10, Wednesday; an image of Shri Sambhavanatha, dedicated by Bai Phulkuvara (*RPLS*, 461, Radhanpur)
11. Samvat 1971, Mahasudi 5, Wednesday; an image of Padmaprabhu, Kunthunatha and Chandraprabhu dedicated by Ben Nathi of Vishanagara; founded by Shah. Jethabhai Deepchanda. (*Shat*, 573, Shatrunjaya)

Many women of this period prefer not to use any familial attribute of identity at all. Instead, they identified themselves using only their personal names. Some other attribution such as caste, place of origin etc., have also been mentioned. Many of them also use the religious attributes *shravika* or *sushravika*.

Most of these records are brief and business like. The place of the majority of such records is Radhanpur. A few are found at Shatrunjaya and other places.

The shortage of engraving space does not seem to be the reason for not giving the name of husband or father. As can be seen, many other details have been given, which in the opinion of the donors were more important. If they wished, they could have easily furnished us with the names of their husbands or fathers or both. Probably, the use of only personal name as a mark of ones identity indicates that the women concerned did not observe the patriarchal norms while constructing their identity. To that extent, they showed independent thinking.

One record that is different from the above records is citation (8). The record informs us that a group of *shravikas* from Darbhati together have donated the image of Shrivasupujya. The donation has been made to mark the end of *Rohini tapa*, a kind of penance. We have noted one inscription of this type in the last chapter too. It seems that the Jaina women came together for religious purposes. As noted in the last chapter, these groups of *shravikas* must have also served as the means of socialisation for the women.

## Women renouncers

> Samvat 1856, Kartika shudi 13; three sets of foot impressions (*paduka*), of *sadhvi* Jirajasiriji, *sadhvi* Chandanabalaji and *sadhvi* Devasiriji, at the base of Mount Siddhachala; sponsored by *muni* Dhiravijaya. (*Shat*, 499, Shatrunjaya)

For this period, only one record could be spotted in which nuns find mention. According to this record *muni* Dhiravijaya, sponsored the *padukas* or the foot impressions of three *sadhvis*. Rajsiriji, Candanabalaji and Devsiriji.

The record is unique on account of its unconventional character. In Jaina monastic discipline, women renouncers, however senior in age and length of initiation and learned in the doctrine, occupy an inferior position to male renouncers, even if they are younger and less scholarly. The fact that *muni* in the present record is sponsoring or financing the foot impressions of three *sadhvis* therefore acquires an overwhelming importance.

In the last chapter, a few epigraphs of period II in which nuns found mention had been noted, and the fact of prescribed rules being followed in letter and spirit was noted too. For period III, if we go by the number of records in which nuns find mention, we are greatly disappointed, as there is only one such record. However, if the contents of the record are considered, it is heartening to note that there were at least a few nuns, who by virtue of their merit commanded respect from all, including the monks.

## Pattern of women's inscriptions

As far as the familial attributes of identity are concerned, during this period, though the majority of the women preferred their wifely attribute there were also many women who preferred not to use any familial attribute at all. They just gave their personal names. The percentage of such women was nearly 36. The percentage of women using their wifely attribute was nearly 43, and percentage of women using their daughterly attribute was only 13, while 4 per cent women used both the attributes, wifely as well as daughterly. The rest of the women used some other attribute of familial identity. The other attributes of identity used by the women were their caste and place of origin and in rare cases the feminine form of the professional attribute and the religious attribute *shravika*.

Most women donated small objects like images or *siddhachakra*, while a few donated for objects like *dehari* (small shrines), which required medium level investment. Only three women gave big donations. Of these, Shiva was of caste Nema while Harkunvar *shethani* and Ujamba were from Osvala caste.

The majority of the women donors came from Shrimali caste, followed by Osvala caste. A few other castes like Pragvat, Nema and others also find mention.

## Comparison between the patterns of men's and women's inscriptions

It has been observed that many men and women of this period opted not to use any familial attribute of identity. The influence of patriarchy on men and women, as reflected in the identification pattern, seems to be less than the same for the previous periods.

As in the previous periods, majority of the men and women donated for small objects like images. The number of men as well as women giving big donations was very less, but the number of men giving big donations was much more than the number of women giving big donations. Largely, the patterns of men's and women's inscriptions are similar.

## Gender relations in period III

Inscriptions of this period, both of men as well as women, are brief and business like and give us very little information on the gender-relations of this period.

Very few women as mothers find mention in the men's inscriptions. This is because firstly, as very few men identify themselves with reference to both the parents, mention of mothers as attribute of men's identity appears in only a few records. This is in contrast to period II, when women as mothers found mention in almost all men's records as the attribute of their identity. Secondly, as the clause indicating the beneficiary of donation is not given in most of the records, mothers as the beneficiaries of men's donations also do not find mention in the men's records. Similarly, in the women's records also, men as sons find mention very rarely. Overall, therefore, these epigraphic records are unable to throw much light on the mother-son relationship. However, from the few records in which mothers find mention, it can be inferred that mothers were respected by their sons as before.

Women as wives also rarely find mention in the men's records. However, in women's records, husbands find mention as the attribute of their identity. This indicates subordination of women to their husbands. Epigraphic records of this period attest to the presence of polygamy, indicating that women continued to be considered as possessions.

The percentage of group donations, which was very high in period II, went down to around ten per cent in period III. This suggests that men and women came together on very few occasions for activities such as making religious donations.

Some of the important observations made in this chapter are summed up below.

High visibility of women as donors is an important feature of this period. The percentage of women donors is higher than the other two periods, and is the highest for the 18th century, which strangely enough was the period of political instability and economic insecurity. It is true that majority of the women preferred their wifely attribute. However, the percentage of women not using any familial attribute was not less either. Therefore, it seems that while identifying themselves a good number of women were less governed by the patriarchal norms. However, in various other aspects of life the influence of patriarchal norms seems to be as strong as that in the previous periods.

The members of a patriarchal joint family consisted of the male head of the family, his wife, sons, daughters-in-law, grandsons and unmarried daughters. Married daughters did not form the part of this family. However, sometimes in epigraphic records married daughters find mention but singly. The names of their husbands and children were never included in this list. Thus, a son-in-law and his children were always considered as outsiders. Even according to the prescriptions of Jaina law, a son-in-law is considered as an outsider. It is said that "The son-in-law, the sister's son and the mother-in-law are never heirs because they are of a different *gotra*".[24] On the whole, therefore, in this respect there was no dichotomy between theory and practice.

Polygamy continued to persist during this period and the co-wives were expected to maintain cordial relations. There are a few records, which show that women indeed tried to fulfil this expectation. For instance, Shiva not only mentioned her elder co-wife in her record but also eulogised her. Similarly, Bai Ajaba and Mankunvar donated in association with each other. They used their motherly attribute to identify themselves and called themselves mothers of Pitamar not letting us know who his biological mother was.

Concepts of masculine and feminine seem to be quite clear. As is evident in Harkunvar *shethani's* record, some qualities were attributed to males, while others were considered as purely feminine qualities. It was thought that women were not capable of taking up complicated tasks outside home. Harkunvar has been praised for accomplishing a task that was masculine in nature.

According to the Jaina law women as a rule could not inherit property or have a share of the property at the time of partition. However, if a woman was the only daughter of her parents she could inherit their property, or else if she was the eldest widow, she as the first heir of her husband's property, could inherit.[25] But it seems that this right of a widow was at times overruled, as was probably done in case of Jadavabai.[26]

Jaina community consists of monks, nuns, laymen and laywomen. Out of these monks, laymen and laywomen are well represented, but the nuns hardly ever find mention in the epigraphic records. The inferior status given to nuns vis-à-vis monks is thus highlighted.

Thus, we note that the Jaina society of Gujarat of period III was largely governed by the patriarchal norms. However, a few cases that varied from the norms are noticeable. These could be treated as exceptional.

Women's financial power was much less than that of men and therefore fewer women made big donations. Nevertheless, rich women's financial power was quite considerable. At times they donated large sums of money. Three women who gave big donations were Bai Shiva, Harkunwar *shethani* and Ujamba. Harkunwar was a widow and thus was probably the inheritor of her husband's property. Shiva was a married woman, but whether she was a widow or not is not known. Ujamba's marital status is not known.

In the inscriptions pertaining to period III, nuns have found mention in only one record. In this record, we find a monk sponsoring or financing the foot impressions of three *sadhvis*. Thus, this record is important because of its unconventional character.

As mentioned in the beginning of the chapter, social reform movements had started in Gujarat after the establishment of the British rule. These movements gained momentum in the second half of the 19th century. The results of these activities were not visible immediately but they did bring about a change in the mindset of at least a few people. As most of the epigraphic records of the 19th century belong to the first half of that century, the changes are not reflected in these records. Even in those few records that belong the second half of the century, such a change is not noticeable. The sources referred to here are mainly of the religious nature and therefore they give information only about the religious donations made by the Jainas. The donations made by the Jaina men and women to the secular institutions such as schools, particularly the female schools; hospitals etc., are not covered by these sources. Another point is that the reform movement did not intend to change the patriarchal framework of the society. What it intended was to expand, to an extent, the space given to women and bring about a few humanitarian changes in their lives. It is, therefore, unreasonable to expect even slight change in the patriarchal pattern of the epigraphic records considered here.

## Notes

1. R.L. Raval, *Socio-Religious Movements in Gujarat (during 19th c).* (New Delhi: Ess Ess Publications, 1987), p. 20.
2. Ibid., p. 35.
3. Ibid., pp. 233–34.
4. Ibid., p. 64.
5. Ibid., pp. 115–19.
6. Kunjalata Shah, "Harkunvar Shethani (1820–1876): A Pioneer in Women's Education in Gujarat", in *University Research Journal,* XXII (2000–2001), S.N.D.T. Women's University, Mumbai, p. 26.
7. R.L. Raval, op. cit., pp. 185, 241.
8. Ibid., pp. 216–22.
9. Ibid., p. 244.

10. The names of Hemabhai's ancestors and their titles match with those given by Commissariat in his book *A History of Gujarat*, Vol. II. The time period is also appropriate. Therefore, in my opinion, the Shantidasa of this record and the Shantidasa mentioned in Commissariat's book is the same person. There is also a record of Shantidasa in *Shat* no. 162. This record is partly mutilated.
11. Acharya Kanchansagarsuri, author and comp., *Shat*, Inscription no. 160.
12. M.S. Commissariat, *A History of Gujarat*, Vol. II (Bombay: Orient Longmans, 1957), p. 140.
13. Ibid., pp. 417, 420.
14. Ibid., p. 510 and Kunjalata Shah, op. cit., p. 23. More about Hatesingh and his wives is described under the heading 'Women with wifely attributes of identity' in the same chapter.
15. G. Buhler, "The Jaina Inscriptions from Shatrunjaya", in *Epigraphia Indica*, Vol. II (1894).
16. See Chapter III, under the heading, 'Women with wifely attributes of identity'.
17. Champat Rai Jain, *The Jaina Law* (Madras: The Devendra Printing and Publishing Co. Ltd., 1926), p. 184.
18. Kunjalata Shah, op. cit., pp. 23–24.
19. Ibid., pp. 4 and 5.
20. See Chapter III *Sati* inscription.
21. Acharya Kanchansagarsuri, op. cit., Part I, p. 142.
22. See in the same chapter under the heading, 'Hemabhai's inscription'.
23. Champat Rai Jain, op. cit., pp. 57, 178. As stated in *Arhanniti*, the brothers should give a fourth share for the purpose of her marriage. But what should be done if the sister never marries is not clear. The other law givers (Digambaras) have prescribed that unmarried sisters be given a share (p. 57).
24. Champat Rai Jain, op. cit., p. 200.
25. Ibid., p. 178, 179, 189.
26. See in the same chapter the explanation of Hemabhai's inscription.

# 5

# Women in Literature and Epigraphy

## A Comparative Perspective

Human beings are generally bound by the rules of the society in which they live. The social norms, the religious prescriptions and proscriptions, and the rules of law, define, to a great extent, the lives of the people. In case of pre-modern India, these three were not exactly separable. In fact, religion touched upon every aspect of life. It played an important part in the lives of all Indians.

'Dharma', the Indian counterpart of religion, refers to a proper course of action in a particular context.[1] It is a "sacred law and duty, justice, religious merit—one of the most comprehensive and important terms in the range of Sanskrit literature. Indian commentators have explained it as denoting an act, which produces the quality of soul called *apurva*, the cause of heavenly bliss and of final liberation. In ordinary usage however, it has a far wider meaning and may denote established practices or customs of any caste or community".[2]

In Jainism, dharma, in addition to the commonly understood meaning, also stands for an eternal substance (*drawya*), the medium that allows beings to move.[3] However, as far as this study is concerned, the term *dharma* refers to the first meaning of dharma, rather than the second.

During the period between 5th century C.E. to 12th century C.E., although the basic assumptions of Jainism remained the same, changes took place in its rituals. The essential change that took place during this period is its transformation from a philosophy, a *darshana,* to a religion, a *dharma*.[4]

Jaina thinkers have prescribed rules of conduct and duties of both renouncers and laypersons. These rules are designed to achieve the main aim or object in life, which according to Jainism is to obtain *moksha* or liberation from the endless cycle of births and deaths. The Jaina discipline is characterised by stages leading to total renunciation.

The householder's life has been divided into eleven stages or *pratimas*. These stages form a series of duties and performances, finally leading to monkhood. When a layperson consistently observes the rules of conduct prescribed for the householders, he/she is qualified to become an ascetic.[5] Both the laypersons and the renouncers have to follow the same *vratas*. In the observance of the *vratas,* householders are given some concession but strict observance is expected from ascetics. The householders are supposed to understand the spirit behind the *vratas* and bring them into action as much as possible.[6]

It is intended in this chapter to see from the literary sources what way of life was prescribed by the Jaina thinkers for its female adherents and compare it with the data collected from the epigraphic sources.

Jaina literature begins with the last of the *tirthankaras,* Lord Mahavira, who reorganised the old Nirgrantha sect and revitalised its moral and religious zeal.[7] The systematic compilation of the teachings of Lord Mahavira in *sutra* form is attributed to *ganadharas* or the chief disciples of the master. He exposed to his eleven *ganadharas* the essence of the doctrine.[8] Unfortunately, the knowledge of these texts was gradually lost, and only a single *ganadhara* could hand it down to the posterity. In the subsequent period, three councils were held to collect and collate the extant portions of the canon. The first one was held at Pataliputra in the 3rd century B.C.E. The second was held at Mathura in the 4th century C.E. under the presidentship of Arya Skandila.

Simultaneously, another council was summoned at Valabhi under the presidentship of Nagarjunasuri in which the canons were fixed. Again, in the beginning of the 6th century C.E., the third council was held once again at Valabhi under the presidentship of Devaradhigani Ksamashramana in which all the important works of the Jainas then available, were written down. The scriptures compiled by this council are generally known as *Agama* or *Siddhanta,* divided into twelve *Angas,* (out of which the twelfth is lost), twelve *Upangas,* ten *Prakirnakas,* six *Cheyasuttas (Chedasutras)* four *Mulasuttas (Mulasutras)* and two miscellaneous texts.[9] Digambaras regard the Shvetambara canon as wholly spurious, though, like Shvetambaras they also hold that the original canon of the Jainas consisted of twelve *Angas.* *Shatakhandagama,* composed by Pushpadanta and Bhutabali in the first or second century C.E., and *Kashaya-Pahuda* of Gunadharacharya, composed about the same time, are the supreme authority for Digambaras regarding the teachings of Mahavira.[10]

Twelve *angas* of Shvetambaras are:[11]

1. *Acharanga*—deals with the life of monks. It furnishes us with materials pertaining to the life of Lord Mahavira.
2. *Sutrakritanga* deals with the refutation of heretical doctrines.
3. *Sthananga*
4. *Samavayanga*
5. *Vyakhyaprajnapti* deals with all types of topics-philosophical, ethical, epistemological and the like. It throws light on the lives of Lord Mahavira, Goshala, Jamali and many others. It is also called as Bhagavati.
6. *Jnatadharmakatha* has various narratives having a moral purpose for its subject matter.
7. *Upasakadasha* consists of ten chapters giving the lives of ten principal lay votaries (upasakas) of the Lord.
8. *Antakriddasha* gives the lives of some liberated souls.
9. *Anuttaraupapatikadasha* deals with the lives of some persons who were born as gods after death.

10. *Prashnavyakarana* consists of ten chapters. The first five deal with *ashrava* (influx of karmic matter) and the last five with *samvara* (stoppage of the influx).
11. *Vipakashruta* deals with the fruits of bad deeds and those of good deeds.
12. *Drishtivada* (not extant)

Historically speaking, the period ascribed to the Shvetambara canon does not seem to go beyond the 6th century C.E. But taking into account that canon were merely redacted in the third council and tradition ascribes the origin of the texts not only to the Pataliputra council but even further back to Mahavira and his chief disciples, it could possibly be said that the earliest portion of the canon belongs to the period of the first disciples of Mahavira or at least to the period of Pataliputra council, i.e., 3rd century B.C.E., while the latest portions possibly belong to the time of Devaradhi, i.e., 6th century C.E.

*Jnatadharmakatha*, the sixth *Anga*, is the most important *Anga* from the point of view of the women's history. In this *Anga* the importance of self-control, austerities, sacrifice etc., has been explained with the help of stories and illustrations. The character sketches of some women like Dharini, Bhadra *sarthavahi*, Devadatta *ganika*, *shravika* Thavacca, Rohini, princess Malli, Pottila, Nagashri, Sukumarika and Draupadi furnish us with a few role models for women of Jaina society.[12]

## Canonical commentaries[13]

Various authors have variously explained the canonical texts in different times. These are mainly of four categories: *Niryuktis, Bhashyas, Churnis and Vrttis*. *Niryuktis* are in verse and are composed by Bhadrabahu in 5th century C.E. Their language is Prakrit. *Bhasyas* are also in Prakrit and in verse. Jinabhadra and Sanghadasagani (6th century C.E.) are well known for their *Bhasyas*. *Churnis* are in Prakrit mixed with Sanskrit. Jinadasagani *mahattara* (7th century C.E.) is the author of most of the *Churnis*. The *Vrttis* are in Sanskrit. Haribhadrasuri, Shilankasuri, Shantyacharya, Abhayadevasuri Maladhari Hemachandra are some of the authors who have composed *Vrittis* from eighth century onwards. There are canonical commentaries in some modern languages too.

In these commentaries, we get references of the persons and events belonging to the canonical period as well as to the contemporary period. We also get some such references, which are found neither in the canonical literature nor in the contemporary period. For instance Marudevi, Brahmi, Sundari and some other women, who find mention in the commentaries, are either not mentioned in the canonical texts or find just a brief mention. It is quite possible that the authors picked them up from some previously existing source or from the traditional accounts.[14]

### *Puranas and Charitas*

The *Mahapurana* by Jinasena and Gunabhadra (9th century C.E.) is the earliest Jaina *Purana*. It contains biographies of sixty-three great men. These are Digambara works. Similar works by Shvetambara authors are called *Charitas*.[15]

### *Other important authors and their works (mainly Shvetambara)*

Umasvati's (known as Umasvamin by Digambaras)[16]: most important work is *Tattvarthadigama sutra*, belonging to an early century of the Common Era. It is the first Sanskrit work on Jaina philosophy, and is recognised by Shvetambaras and Digambaras both.[17]

Siddhasena Divakara was a great logician, also belonging to one of the early centuries of the Common Era. He too is regarded by both the sects as their own.

Uddyotanausri composed *Kuvalayamala* in 779 C.E. He belonged to the Shvetambara sect.[18]

Hemachandra (1089 C.E.-1172 C.E.) was the most versatile and prolific Jaina writer of Sanskrit. He was called the omniscient of the Kali age (*Kalikalasarvajna*). He was a Gujarati whose patrons were the Caulukya kings Jayasimha Siddharaja and Kumarapala. He has composed books on grammar, logic, history, polity and so on. Some of his important works are

*Kavyanushasana*, an excellent work on rhetoric; *Dvyashrayakavya* (poem with double purpose); *Trishashtishalakapurushacharita*, the lives of sixty-three great men; *Yogashastra,* an important work on Jaina yoga, and *Arhanniti or Laghvarhanniti*, a valuable treatise on Jaina polity.[19]

*Dvyashrayakavya* aims at explaining the grammatical treatise called *Haimashabdanushasana* written by the poet himself. Twenty cantos of the book are written in Sanskrit and eight cantos are written in Prakrit. The Prakrit portion is also called *kumarapalacarita,* because the annals of only Kumarpala are found in this. The first twenty cantons describe the Caulukya dynasty and the life of King Jayasimha. The rules of Sanskrit grammar are illustrated in this part. The second part explains the ruler of Prakrit grammar. There are some references to queens and other royal women in *Dvyashrayakavya*. These references, help us in forming an opinion about the author's views on women. *Trishashtishalakapurushacharita* is one of the most important works of Hemachandra, as far as the writing of women's history is concerned. While narrating the stories of the great men the author has also given the detailed description of the incidents related to the mothers, wives and other female relatives of the great men. The customs, social practices, attitude of the society towards women are all reflected in these descriptions.

*Arhanniti* is the only Shvetambara work on Jaina law. The other existing sources of Jaina law—*Bhadrabahu Samhita, Vardhamana Niti, Indranandi Jina Samhita, Trivarnikachara* and the *Adipurana*—are all authored by Digambara authors.[20] Hemachandra, in the colophon of *Arhanniti,* declares that he had reduced to writing what he had heard.[21] In the light of the above information, it is very difficult to say whether Jaina law was used by the Jainas of Gujarat or not. However, as Hemachandra was the author of *Arhaniti,* it is very likely that from the 12th century C.E. onwards Jaina law and customs were in use among the Jainas of Gujarat. Nevertheless, by mid or late 19th century, British courts had started applying the Hindu law to the Jainas when cases were brought to the court. On many occasions the courts tried to ascertain Jaina law or at least Jaina customs, so that the dispute of Jainas may be decided according to their own rules. However, when they did not get access to these laws, they started enforcing Hindu laws on the Jainas from the 19th century. This was because the Jaina pandits were not ready to produce their scriptures in the courts. "In the past a long series of vicissitudes and persecutions drove the light of Jainism underground and behind barred doors. When the British came, the Jainas concealed their *Shastras* and objected to their production in the courts".[22]

*Arhanniti* is thus an important source book for the laws related to the Shvetambara Jaina women.

Merutungacharya: Merutungacharya of Vardhamanapura composed *Prabandhachintamani* in 1305 C.E. Though it is an account of Kumarapala and his successors, it also contains the stories of some other kings like Vikramarka, Satavahana king and others. According to the author, he composed *Prabandhachintamani* for two reasons. Firstly, as the old stories of *Ramayana* and *Mahabharata* did not interest the intelligent men anymore, he felt the need for a new book, which would inform the people about the great men of the recent past. Secondly, the book would also benefit the future generations of intelligent men.[23]

Like *Trishashtishalakapurushacharita*, this book also describes the events related to women, the queens, princesses, wives of ministers and even a few ordinary women, and thus is useful for the reconstruction of women's history.

Yashovijaya was a great scholar and monk of Gujarat belonging to the17th century C.E. He was a prolific writer who composed in Sanskrit, Prakrit, Gujarati and Rajasthani. Some of his important works are *Jnanasara, Aadhyatmasara, Jaina Tarkabhasha, Devadharmapariksha* and others.[24] As most of these works are on Jaina philosophy and logic, they have a limited use for this study.

For the modern period too, scholarly works on various aspects of Jainology are not wanting. Jacobi was one of the pioneering scholars of the modern period whose contribution to Jaina literature is immense. He has translated some of the canonical texts like *Ayaranga, Kappasutta* and *Suyagudanga*, for the *Sacred Books of the East* series (SBE) in the late 19th century.

There is also another kind of Jaina literature of the modern period. This literature is meant not for the scholars but for the lay followers of the Jaina religion. Such works are generally composed in vernaculars. These works are more important for this study as they give us a glimpse of the contemporary socio-religious practices and norms. One such booklet written in Gujarati is *Jaina Stri Sadbhodha: Sannario mate Amulya Upadesha.*[25] The booklet was first published in the second decade of the 20th century. Its second reprint was published in 1931 and the third in 1933. This is a manual of instructions meant generally for women and particularly for Jaina women. The influence of the reform movements of the 19th century is visible in the contents of this booklet. The booklet aims at bringing about a change in the lives of Jaina women in order to make them good housewives. The author believes that the well-being of the family depends upon the lady of the house, and therefore educating girls to become good housewives is essential. Though the booklet was first published in the second decade of the 20th century, the values, which find expression in it had already started taking shape in the mid-19th century. This is indicated by the fact that the leading families of wealthy traders and financiers who directly or indirectly encouraged the reform movement at the initial stage, hailed from the Jaina community.[26] The above mentioned work is being used as the representative of the 19th century values.

This was only a brief survey of Jaina literature, which is very vast. Jainas have produced literature touching upon almost all aspects of human life such as religion, philosophy, art, history and so on. It is not possible even to mention all of them in this place.

Some authors have used the canonical literature and its commentaries for the study of the position of women. They include, among others, Vilas Sangave,[27] Sagarmal Jain,[28] Hirabai Boradiya[29] and Nalini Joshi.[30] Drawing from these works, it is intended to see what were the norms and practices, which governed the lives of women mentioned in the canonical literature. These will serve as the primordial norms. The literature of the subsequent period will help in noting the changes, if any, in these norms.

## Women in Jaina literature

Jainas, like the Hindus, show an ambivalent attitude towards women. "Right in the earliest portion of the canon, a woman is looked upon as something evil that enticed innocent males into a snare of misery. They are described as the 'greatest temptations', 'the cause of sinful acts', 'the slough', 'demons' etc. Their bad qualities are described in exaggerated terms. Their passions are said to destroy the celibacy of monks" like pot filled with lac near fire".[31]

"Jaina texts in the voice of Manu, state that a woman while a child must be kept under the control of her father, when married under her husband, when a widow under her son. A woman is never allowed to live independently".[32]

In the praise of a woman, it is said that the glory of a virtuous woman is spread in the world. They are worshipped by Gods and men alike. Women giving birth to *tirthankaras, chakravartins, vasudevas, baldevas* are worship worthy. The chaste women and virtuous wives are specially praised and it is said that the virtuous women are capable of giving curse or showing favour.[33]

Though these statements seem contradictory, they are actually two sides of the same coin. Only those women, who lived under subordination to men and were virtuous, were praised. Likewise, women giving birth to great men were also praised. They became great by the deeds of their sons. But that is what patriarchal value system is. In pre-modern India, men and women were indoctrinated into the system held sacrosanct. The women, in return for protection from other males, accepted the logic of the system and adhered to it even when it oppressed and exploited them. It is only recently, that too to some extent, that patriarchy is being challenged. This was the general attitude towards women.

### *Daughter*

In the canons girls and unmarried daughters were referred to by different names like *kanna, duya* or *darika*.[34] However, in the epigraphs, which come from a much later period, we do not come across these terms. Instead the Sanskrit terms *duhita, suta* and *putri* are found. It seems this was because of the preference for Sanskrit over Prakrit.

The Jaina canons have us believe that daughters were not unwelcome. Childless women wished for a son or a daughter. In *Jnatadharmakatha*, Dhanyaa, wife of Dhanya *sarthavaha*, prays in front of the images of Yaks's, Naga, Kubera etc. and says that "If I beget son or daughter I will increase your treasure and worship you". The kings, the *sarthavahas*, that is the merchants or leaders of the caravan, and ordinary people celebrated the birth of a daughter also.[35] In Jainism a son was not necessary to attain *moksha,* which was the case among Hindus. According to the teachings of *tirthnkaras* each individual is responsible for his/her own spiritual progress.[36] Many of the Jaina *tirthankaras* were sonless, and yet they attained *moksa.*[37] However, all this should not lead us to believe that sons and daughters were preferred equally. For earning money and for maintaining the familial order, a son was required and therefore sons were preferred more than the daughters were.

Relations between father and daughter were those of affection. Fathers used to think of the happiness of their daughters. Those girls who were not desirous of getting married continued to stay with their fathers. After the death of the father, brothers took over the responsibility of their sisters. When the daughters attained youth, their fathers would become aware of getting them married. Many times, she was consulted about her marriage. All such references suggest that child marriage was not in vogue in the period of the canon.[38] In the later centuries also it seems that the princesses were not married in childhood but no information is available about the ordinary girls. However, Abhyatilakagani, commentator on *Dvayashrayakavya,* has indicated that marriage of girls had become a headache for fathers.[39] During the Muhammadan period, the Jainacharyas prescribed the age of twelve years for girls and sixteen years for boys as the marriageable age, giving the reason of *apattikala.*[40] It seems that this practice was continued even in the beginning of 20th century.[41]

Education of girls during the canonical period was not neglected altogether. *Jnatadharmakatha* refers to seventy-two arts for men and sixty-four arts for women, but whereas the seventy-two arts of men are described in detail, the sixty-four arts for women find a mere mention.[42] That the highborn girls and princesses were given good education is suggested by references in *Prabandhachintamani*. For instance, it is mentioned that Priyagumanjiri, daughter of Vikramaditya of Malva, was highly educated. The responsibility of her education was entrusted to *pandita* Vararuchi. Being intelligent, she completed the learning of all sciences in a few day's time. However, for ordinary people, it seems that education of girls was not a priority. In fact later on many Jainas, like their Hindu counterparts, believed that educating women was an act against *dharma*.[43] But still later, under the influence of the reform movements of the 19th century, women's education began to be advocated. Yet educating girls did not mean that they were to be given education like the boys. The author of *Jaina Stri Sadbodha* makes it clear that by women's education he means education useful to *stri-dharma*.[44] The curriculum prescribed for girls was—reading, writing and utilitarian education relating to home or housekeeping. Along with this, religious education was also prescribed.[45] The author further adds that the curriculum for girls and boys has to be different because girls do not have to go out to take up a job or engage in business. The author has quoted from the Jaina religious books in order to convince people that in the past *Jainacharyas* had favoured girls' education. He feels that if the girls are not educated, then their going to *upashrayas* for hearing sermons is of no use, as they will not understand *dharma*.

Thus, it seems that during the canonical period, daughters, though second in importance after their brothers, were taken good care of, and were given some education also. However Jaina girls gradually lost their right to education, which they regained, to a limited extent, only in the 20th century.

## Property rights of daughters

According to the Jaina law, a daughter generally was not considered as heir to the property.[46] If after the death of the father, there were one or more unmarried daughters (of his), it was stipulated that their marriages should be performed by the brothers by giving a fourth from their share.[47]

Only in exceptional cases, the daughters had a right to property. These were:

1. If a person died leaving one daughter and no other children, the daughter and her son became master of the estate. This provision is similar to the one in Hindu law, according to which a sonless father could appoint his daughter as *putrika,* so that her son would offer pindas as a son, to his maternal grandfather.[48] The term *putrika* though could not be located in the Jaina law, but in Jaina epigraphs of period I and II the use of the term can be noted.
2. Another occasion when daughter could inherit their father's property was when a sonless widow, who had inherited the property of her husband did not adopt a son. In such a situation her daughter became the mistress of the entire estate.[49]

From the above provisions it is not clear what would happen if a couple had no sons, but had more than one daughter. Both of these provisions of Jaina law were also practised in actual life, as is clear from the epigraphic evidences. For instance—Somi who donates the image of Shantinatha in V.S 1303 calls herself *putrika* of Chandra.[50] A man, Virsingh, who donated along with his wife and daughter in V.S 1573 refers to his daughter as *putrika.*[51] Thus, the epigraphic evidences show that the only daughters of sonless fathers could in fact inherit their father's property through their sons. This term has also been used in epigraphs by some of the women donors for their daughters.

Daughters figure very rarely in the epigraphic records of men as well as women, either as the beneficiaries of donations or as the associate donors. However, many women chose to identify themselves by using their daughterly status up to the 14th century. After the 14th century, we find that fewer and fewer women preferred to identify themselves in terms of their daughterly status, while the proportion of women preferring to identify themselves as wives grew larger simultaneously. Perhaps, the importance of daughters in the family was reduced after the 14th century or else women's role in the family as wives came to be regarded as more important. May be it was because they became less dependent on their fathers.

### *Wife*

Jainas give utmost importance to asceticism and the institution of marriage has been accepted as one, which would aid in the practice of celibacy. Marriages are considered essential only for those who are not in a position to practice complete celibacy.[52]

*Panigrahana* is the term used for marriage in canons. The parents or elder brother mostly fixed the marriages of the young girls and boys, but there are also examples where girls exercised their choice. *Kula,* vansha, profession and financial position were the considerations for fixing marriages. There are many example of *inter-varna,* both *auloma* and *pratiloma*, and inter sect marriages in the canonical literature.[53] this is in contrast to the Jaina practices of the 20th century. By this time Jainas were divided into many endogamous castes and subcastes.[54] However, society, as envisaged by Lord Parshvanatha, Lord Mahavira and other *acharyas* was a society in which classes, i.e., *varnas* were not watertight compartments. For them it was a social practice, unconnected with religion. These classes were based on the professions, which people followed and not on birth. However, later on many castes and sub castes developed from the four *varnas*.[55]

From the epigraphical evidence it seems that the practice of marrying a person only from one's own caste must have become fairly common among the Jainas in the thirteenth century itself. It can be noted that Tejapala and Vastupala had married girls of their own caste. Of course, one epigraphic record also tells us that Tejapala, in the latter years of his life, probably after the death of his first wife, had married a girl of another caste.[56]

In Hindu *Smriti* literature we come across eight forms of marriage, namely *brahma, daiva, arsha, prajapatya, asura, gandharva, rakshasa* and *paishacha.* No reference to *svayamvara* is found. In the Jaina *Agamas* we do not come across these names, but it seems *brahma* (marriages fixed by parents), *asura, prajapatya* and *svayamvara* were the four types of marriages popular among them.[57]

Polygamy was prevalent among the rich and royals from very ancient times right up to the 19th century. This reduced the importance of women and made them objects of possession. In canon, we find examples of kings who had not only many but numerous wives. The chief queen of a *chakravartin* was considered as one of the fourteen gems. She was the first *stri-ratna.*[58]

We find many examples of rivalry between the co-wives.[59] In Hemachandra's *TSPC*, at many places, women were depicted as mere objects of possession. For example, "There in the city of Kanchanpura, possessing golden splendour excelling Bhogavati, Amarpuri, Lanvea etcetera." Its king was Vikramayashasa, whose power was excellent, the lightning of whose splendour increased the rain of the tears of his enemy's wives. *There are five hundred gazelle-eyed women in his household, objects of affection, like cow elephants of an elephant, who is the lord of herd*" (emphasis added).[60]

The married life of women in polygamous marriages must have been miserable and could have sometimes encouraged illicit relations.[61] The relations between husband and wife in monogamous marriages might have been happier. In canonical literature there are many examples when husband and wife took decisions together. They addressed each other respectfully using the terms, *devanupriye* and *devanupriya*. The use of the terms *arye* and *aryaputra* occurs rarely.[62]

The epigraphic records amply attest to the prevalence of polygamy. Just to cite a few examples, starting from period I, Tejapala and Vashipala, the two ministers had two wives each. Dhanasiri and Vanade, the women donors of period II, call themselves second wife of their respective husbands'.[63] *Nagarshetha* Vakhatchand (period III) had two wives. Some of his sons also had more than one wife each.[64]

Married women were expected to take upon themselves the responsibility of household work such as cooking, cleaning, serving in-laws, looking after the children and so on. These were the duties, which all Indian women, irrespective of religion, were expected to perform. There were also a few duties of married women, which were specific to Jaina women like cooking food that the monks and nuns could consume and offering alms to them, and taking care of potable water. Water pots had to be cleaned and water had to be strained and stored.[65] A virtuous and obedient wife was considered praiseworthy. Hemachandra praised those qualities of a women which made her good wife. Thus, he says about the mother of Mallinatha, "Purifying the whole earth by her spotless wifehood, the source of happiness, she shone like a living *tirtha*".[66]

The duties of a wife are summed up in a Sanskrit verse.[67] The translation of the same is given below:

"She should be able to give advice like a minister, while working should be like a mother, in the bedroom be like a nymph, should help in religious duties and should be able to endure all sorrows and joys like the earth."

A wife was expected to serve her husband and in-laws always. Women were also expected to be considerate towards their co-wives and never be jealous of them.

That these ideals were in reality also cherished by the Jaina women is shown by the epigraphic records. Co-wives come together for donating in quite a few records. For instance, a record at Abu, says that Bilhanadevi and Dhandaladevi, wives of Vijada, together made the donation.[68] Their coming together to donate shows that the relation between them might have been cordial.

The duties of a married women were many and her rights very few. A woman was expected to perform all the above mentioned duties in return for security and a few property rights.

### *Property rights of wives*

Married woman was entitled to a property known as *stri-dhana*. Whatever ornaments, clothes, vessels and the like were given to a woman at the time of marriage or subsequently by the father, mother, kinsmen, father's brothers, elder sister, father's sister and the like, or by husband or by in-laws was termed as *stri-dhana*.[69] *Stri-dhana* was not liable to partition. The husband was allowed to take the *stri-dhana* only if he did not have any other means, for illness or for religious purpose. However, it was not obligatory for him to refund the same.[70]

Apart from the *stri-dhana*, a married woman was also given some right to property at the time of partition in the ancestral property. Equal shares were given to the sons, to their mothers and to the father, when the partition took place in the lifetime of the father.[71] Even if the partition took place after the death of the father, it was stated that the mother should be given half share by the sons for carrying on the ordinary purpose of the world.[72]

The fact that so many women came out to make donations indicated that women must have possessed some kind of property or assets from which they could make the donations. There is one record in which the woman donor tells us that she is making the donation from her own money.[73]

In the eyes of women, though their role as a wife was their more important role throughout the millennium, but it gained paramount importance in period II, as indicated by the epigraphic records. It can be noted that majority of the women used their wifely attribute to identify themselves. In period I, approximately 43 per cent women used their wifely attribute, while in period II approximately 71 and in period III again approximately 43 per cent preferred this attribute.

From the men's inscriptions it can be observed that in period I, wives found mention in their husbands' inscriptions only occasionally, as the beneficiaries of donations. In period II, wives found mention occasionally as the beneficiaries of their husbands' donations, as well as the associate donors, while in period III, in most of the men's records, their wives did not find mention. Husband and wife associated together for making donations more often in period II.

### Mother

Generally, in all ages, mothers have enjoyed high status. Motherhood was considered auspicious and every married woman looked forward to becoming a mother, especially of son/sons. From the references in the canons, it seems that the mothers took responsibility of their offspring more seriously than the fathers did. We find many instances where the father becomes a monk even while his children were young, and the mother took upon herself the responsibility of the upbringing of her children, including their education and marriage.[74]

That the mothers were respected by their sons is illustrated by the description of the mothers of *tirthankaras*. Sons respected the wishes of their mothers and made efforts to fulfil them. It is said that the mother is the first teacher of her children. The author of *Jaina Stri Sadbodha,* while advocating education for women, says that a child spends most of his time in the company of his mother, and therefore if the mother was virtuous and well educated, then she could positively influence her sons and daughters. Mothers were mainly responsible for moulding the behaviours of their children.[75]

### Property rights of the mothers

It is stated that, "when there is partition after the death of the father the mother should be given a half share by the sons for carrying on ordinary purposes of the world. When she dies, the sons take her share".[76]

In the women's inscriptions, throughout the millennium, their sons found mention occasionally as the beneficiaries of donations. In period II, sons also found mention as the associate donors. In group donations, if a woman was the chief donor, she usually associated her sons (in some cases also daughters-in-law) with her, but sons as the attribute of their mothers' identity found only a rare mention. Throughout the millennium, there are only a few records where women have used their motherly attribute of identity. This indicates either that they were not dependent on their sons or that such a practice did not exist, or both.

A look into the records of men shows that in periods I and III, men sometimes mentioned the names of their mothers alongside the name of the father as the attribute of their identity. However, in period II, men, almost as a rule, always identified themselves with reference to both their parents. In other words, in period II, mothers always found mention as the attribute of their sons' identity. It could be argued that in a polygamous society mention of the name of the mother was necessary. However, it does not seem that this was the only reason for mentioning the mother's name firstly, because all the marriages were not polygamous and secondly, if it were so, they would find mention as the attribute of their sons' identities even in period I and III as well, because polygamy was prevalent in those periods also.

Mothers also sometimes found mention in the record of their sons as the beneficiaries of donations.

From all the above references to the mother-son relationship, it seems that in the familial hierarchy, mothers were at a higher position than their sons were. The respect shown by the sons towards their mothers without the mother holding any real power, was not just a gesture. According to the Jaina law, a woman was the first heir to the property of her husband. The sons were only the next heirs.[77] Thus, even when a woman was not widowed, she held a latent power over her sons. Such must have been the case where the woman was either the first or the only wife of her husband, as it was the eldest wife who was the heir to her husband's property.[78]

### *Widow*

The worst phase of life for a woman was the one in which she had to live the life of a widow. In *Agamas* child widows are referred to. If a widow was of mature age, she was taken care of by her sons or else she became a nun. If the widow was young or was sonless, she would spend the rest of her life in the house of her father or could become a nun. Many a time, after the death of her husband, she would die grief stricken.[79] The widows had to live a plain uneventful life, usually serving the family members. The condition of the widows has been explained very succinctly in *Jnatadharmakatha,* by using an allegorical expression—"tears are her only companions".[80]

Remarriage of a widower was sanctioned, but there is no instance of widow remarriage in the *Agamas*. Though widow remarriage was disapproved by the society, it did occur at times. The mother of Vastupala and Tejapala was a widow who was remarried to their father Asaraja. Though other authors have avoided mentioning this inconvenient fact, Merutungacarya has clearly mentioned it in his *Prabandhachintamani.*[81]

The case of second marriage by a woman while her first husband was alive was unthinkable, but Merutungacharya has recorded a solitary case of this nature. Virdhavala's mother, Madanarajni, had entered into another wedlock even when her first husband Lavanaprasada was alive.[82] Obviously people wielding power and prestige could make as well as break the norms as and when necessary. However, cases such as these are exceptional and how far the women concerned had initiative in the matter can hardly be ascertained.

Many reformers of Gujarat in the latter half of the 19th century were advocating widow remarriage, but the author of *Jaina stri sadbodha* published in early 20th century, is silent about it. On the contrary the quality of being *pativrata* has been emphasised.[83] It seems therefore that some of the Jaina authors were not in favour of widow remarriage.

In India one custom associated with widowhood was that of *sati,* that is burning of a widow on the pyre of her dead husband. This practice was prevalent among the Hindus. In canons there are one or two references to *sati,* but these references are not sufficient to indicate that *sati* was practiced in the Jaina community in India.[84] In *TSPC* of Hemachandra there is one instance that refers to *sati.* In the biography of *vasudeva,* Purusasimha, his mother utters the following words when her husband was on his deathbed, "... I cannot bear hearing the word 'widow', even for a moment, consequently, I wearing safflower shall go ahead of your father. My birth had its purpose accomplished by my husband, King Shiva and by you, a son, the fifth *ardhacakrin* son. At my husband's death my life will depart of its own accord. I shall abandon it by entering the fire".[85] Technically, she would not be a *sati*, as her husband was still living, but it amounts to the same.[86]

This passage does not indicate that Jainism supported the practice of *sati*. Nevertheless, it surely tells us how dreadful widowhood was for women and so they preferred to die rather than live as a widow.

Though Jainism does not support the practice of *sati*, one epigraphic record of *sati* has been noted,[87] which has been cited in Chapter III. The record says that three wives, Rupashri, Koma and Kesarajani of Rupacanda, son of Sonapala and grandson of Rishabhadasa, committed sati in V.S. 1672.

Isolated though the inscription is—it reflects cross-cultural influence, and there is a possibility that a few more cases of the type have gone unrecorded.

Pitiable though the condition of widows was Jaina thinkers tried to reduce their misery, to some extent, by giving them considerable property rights.

### *Property rights of widows*

According to the Jaina law, the wife was the first heir of a deceased person.[88] The *eldest wife*, whether there be a son or not was the mistress of the wealth like her husband.[89] The author of *Arhanniti* had perceived a situation where the husband's death was certain. Therefore, he suggested that such a man could appoint a manager for the preservation of his estate by giving him the appointment in writing, bearing the permission of the king and attestation by witness. If the manager so appointed did not discharge his duties properly after the death of the owner or became antagonistic to the widow of the deceased, then she could dismiss him and could carry on the work with the help of another person trusted by her.[90]

The widow's right to property was accompanied with many responsibilities as it was stated that she should preserve the property in her charge with great care, and support the family by her cleverness.[91]

However, this right to property was not absolute; it came with a tag attached. It was stated that if a widow was perverse or of evil conduct, she should be expelled by the husband's brothers and their sons, after making settlement for her maintenance.[92] Further, if a widow was possessed by an evil spirit or was suffering from a malignant disease or paralysis etc., and was not able to protect the estate or family, she should be supported by her husband's brothers or other stipulated relations, and her wealth should be protected by them with great care.[93]

It seems that a widow got all these rights only when the partition had taken place before the death of her husband. If partition took place after the death of the husband, it was stipulated that she be given half share by her sons for carrying on ordinary purposes of the world.[94]

A widowed daughter-in-law had no right to property left by the father-in-law when the mother-in-law was alive, beyond the right to maintenance.[95]

A woman whose husband was lost or had become distressed in mind or had become a monk, also became the mistress of her husband's property.[96]

Though the Jaina law givers gave widows the right to property, but it seems in the past many kings used to confiscate the property of men who died sonless, and deprived their widows the right to property. We are told that Kumarapala, under the influence of Hemachandracarya, and Akbar, under the influence of Hirvijayasuri, abandoned this practice. Kumarapala took twelve minor vows of a *shravaka*, of these the third vow required a *shravaka* to abstain from stealing. In order to observe this vow he gave up the income from *rudatikara* (property of sonless widow).[97] Similarly, Akbar also respecting the Jaina principles, stopped the practice of confiscating the property of sonless widows.[98]

Only one inscription, that of Harkunvar *sethani,* has been noted, which explicitly states the fact of her husband's death, thereby indicating her widowed status.[99] The inscription tells us that she took over the activities unfinished by her husband. This suggests that she had inherited her husband's property. Other sources indicate that she was the third wife (according to inscription, second) of Hatesingh Kesarsingh, a rich merchant of Ahmedabad. One of her co-wives was alive at the time of the death of her husband but she was blind. This is mentioned in her inscription. Perhaps because of this reason, Harkunvar looked after the affairs of her husband's estate instead of her elder co-wife.

This seems to be the only inscription, which explicitly mentions the widowed state of the donor. The epigraphic records being decontextualised, it is difficult to say how many of the women donors were widows. However, it is quite likely that some women, who were the chief donors of group donations with their sons as associate donors, must have been widows who had inherited their husband's property.

The inscription of Tejalade, where she is the sole donor, does not mention her as a widow. The inscription is dated V.S. 1661. It says that she is donating according to the instructions of her husband. Soni Tejapala (Tejalade's husband) finds mention as the donor in a few inscriptions. The last record in which Tejapala finds mention as the donor is dated V.S. 1659 (JDLS-II, 913). Thus, it seems that at the time of making donation in V.S. 1661, Tejalade was in fact a widow and had inherited her husband's property.[100]

Such references, though only a few, suggest that perhaps the property rights given to the Jaina women in theory, were also given to then in practice, at least in some cases.

## Women and religion

Women were expected to perform some duties towards their family members in the roles of daughters, wives and mothers. Nevertheless, even while performing their household duties the Jaina women could strive for their spiritual progress.

In India, two distinct trends known as *Brahmanic* and *Shramanik* have been prevalent from the earliest days.[101] *Brahmanic* tradition was represented earlier by Vedic tradition and later by Hindu tradition. *Shramanik* tradition has been represented mainly by Jainism and Buddhism.

In the *Brahmanic* tradition, during the Vedic period some women could recite mantras and take part in *yajna*. Some of the verses of the Vedas have been authored by women. During this period they could remain unmarried as *brahmavadinis* or *parivrajikas*, but this group of Vedic renouncers had almost become extinct by the *smriti* period. It began to be emphasised that being a virtuous wife, a *pativrata* serving her lord who was her husband, was the supreme dharma of a woman.[102] Jainism and Buddhism however gave women the right to renounce the world. Jainism's most important schism took place in the beginning of the Common Era when the Jainas split into the Digambaras and Shvetambaras. Though both of them allowed women to become nuns, Digambaras believed that a woman could not attain *moksha*. She had to be reborn as a male to attain *moksha*. However, Shvetambaras believed that a woman was as much capable of attaining *moksha* as a man was.[103]

*Moksa* has been prescribed by Jainism as the goal of human existence. *Samyak darshana* (right faith), *samyak jnana* (right knowledge) and *samyak carita* (right conduct), known as *ratnatraya* (the three jewels) together, constitute the path of salvation.[104] There are two courses of moral conduct according to the Jaina ethics, one prescribed for householders and the other for renouncers. The householders, equipped with the three jewels, must observe the five *vratas* or vows, namely *ahinsa, satya, asteya, brahmacharya* and *aparigraha,* i.e., he/she must be free form cruelty, untruth, theft, unchastity, avarice and unnecessary luxury. They are called *anuvratas*, or the minor code of morals.[105] The householders are also expected to observe three *gunavratas* and four *shikshavratas*. Thus, a householder/*shravaka* or a housewife/*shravika* is supposed to observe twelve *vratas* in all.[106] Apart from these twelve *vratas,* a householder or a housewife has also to pass through eleven stages or grades known as *pratimas,* before he/she can enter the life of an ascetic.[107]

## Shravikas

The guidelines for the householders are given in *Upasakadasha* in the from of stories. The wives of householders or the *shravakas* were called *shravikas.*[108] The Jaina women throughout the period of Jaina history, practiced *dharma* as they understood it and strove for their spiritual progress. *Shravikas* had a firm faith in their religion and they worshipped Jina images. In canons there are examples, which indicate that many a time they were the encouraging force behind their husbands. There are many examples of intelligent and expert orator *shravikas as* well. Jayanti was one such *shravika.* She was the sister of king Shatanika of Kaushambi, and paternal aunt of Udayan. She became a nun and the disciple of Lord Mahavira. In the canon, there are also instances where, if a *shravika* was married to a non-*shravaka*, then such *shravika* would cleverly change the mind of her husband and make him a *shravaka.* Many of these *shravikas* became nuns in their later lives.[109]

There are many examples of devout *shravikas* in literature, who in their own way contributed to the Jaina religion.

Shrimati, wife of minister Vimalasha, the builder of a marvellous temple on Mt. Abu, was a very religious lady. Vimalasha and Shrimati enjoyed all luxuries of life but were childless. On this account, they were very unhappy. According to the oral tradition, once Vimalasha worshipped d*evi Ambika* without taking food or water for three days. Upon this, the *Devi* was pleased and appeared in his dream. She told him to ask for a boon. The minister asked for a son and permission for construction of a temple at Mt. Abu. However, *Devi* was ready to grant only one boon. The minister consulted his wife Shrimati, who in turn opted for a temple. She felt that in this ephemeral world, something that enhances religion was more important. Because of this sacrifice of Shrimati, a marvellous temple was constructed on Mt. Abu in 1032 C.E. She, on account of this sacrifice, is respected in the Jaina tradition.[110]

Another woman who sacrificed her son for religion was Pahini, mother of Hemachandracharya. She gave away her son to *muni* Devachandra to become a monk upon his request.[111]

Minaladevi, mother of King Jaysingh Siddharaja, was a very influential person. Though she was not a Jaina, she was favourable to Jainism and helped in popularising it. She undertook many works for the benefit of the people. Because of her influence, her son King Jaysingh Siddharaja also patronised Jainism, made pilgrimage to Shatraunjaya and donated twelve villages to Adinatha Jinalaya.[112] In 1100 C.E. Minaladevi constructed a lake in village Varuma.

Anupama, wife of Tejapala, to whom reference has been made in Chapter 2, had great influence on her husband; she supervised the construction of a Jina temple at Abu in 1232 C.E. She was also sympathetic to the artisans working for the temple and saw to it that they got all necessary facilities.[113]

In the above examples, Shrimati and Pahini have been praised for sacrificing their sons. Their husbands whose sacrifice was also equally great have not been praised. They have been commended for different reasons. Vimalashah has been praised for constructing a grand temple. Here the role of gender stereotyping can be seen. Since it was thought that women sought worldly pleasures more than men did, therefore, it was thought more difficult for women to sacrifice worldly pleasures. Shrimati and Pahini have been praised for overcoming their desires and helping men in adherence to and propagation of religion. Anupama also played a supportive role. Minaladevi on the other hand took a lead role and helped in popularising Jainism. She also influenced her son.

In the Jaina tradition, the number of *shravikas* has always been more than the *shravakas*, and number of nuns has been more than monks.[114] In the *sangha* of Mahavira, the number of *shravikas* was thrice that of the *shravakas* and in the *sangha* of Mallinatha also, the proportion was approximately the same.[115] However, in the absence of demographic data for the period, there is no source to verify the figures. Only, the data for the contemporary period is available. The census report of 2001 shows that the Jaina population of Gujarat was 5,25,305 (males 2,66,768 and females 2,58,537). This means that the Jaina women are slightly less than Jaina men in Gujarat. It can be said that the number of *shravakas* and *shravikas* presently is nearly equal. It can therefore be presumed that the proportion must have been more or less the same in the past as well.

The visibility of lay Jaina women or *shravikas* in the Jaina epigraphs of Gujarat is quite high. Women find mention as mothers, wives or as the beneficiaries of the donations in many records. However, the occurrence of women donors is comparatively less frequent.

The Jainas considered giving of donations meritorious. Hemachandra advised laypersons to sow their wealth on seven *kshetras*. The two most important *kshetras* were the *Jina* image and the Jaina temples.[116] Women were also allowed to donate, but their power to do so was restricted by many factors like limited property rights and limited opportunities to go out on pilgrimages and make donations. The epigraphic space allowed to women was the least in 13th and 14th centuries and the most in 17th, 18th and 19th centuries (see Table 1 in Chapter 1). On an average women donors occupied only thirteen per cent of the Available epigraphic space. Many *shravikas* about whom we know nothing from the literary sources are made visible by the epigraphic sources. To cite a few names of the women who have made substantial donations, Tejalade contributed for a Jina temple in V.S. 1661; Hirabai renovated the Jina temple in V.S. 1683; and *bai* Shiva contributed for a Jina Prasada at Shatrunjaya in V.S. 1916.

*Shravikas,* even while being householders, could strive for their spiritual development, but Jainism also gave the option of renouncing the world and becoming a nun to women.

## Sadhvis

### *Causes of renunciation*

As in the case of males, so also in the case of females, a variety of reasons led to their renunciation. Women attending the sermons of the *tirthankaras*, motivated by the desire for salvation, embraced the life of a nun. Women belonging even to the higher strata of the society renounced the world. Many women, like Vashisthi, renounced the world when their husbands and sons become monks. Rajimati, hearing the news of her would be husband's renunciation (*tirthankara* Aristanemi), became a nun. Many a time even ordinary causes led to renunciation. Pottila, the wife of a minister, become a nun when she realised that her husband had lost all love for her. For some widowhood became the reason for becoming a nun. Courtesans coming under the spell of religion, became nuns.[117]

For centuries, these have been the factors motivating women to join the order of nuns. Widowhood especially has been one of the important reasons for women to become nuns. However, in recent years the number of women who have never been married but are joining the order is increasing.[118]

The ceremony of renunciation for the nuns did not differ much from that which was carried out in case of the monks. Before entering the order, both men and women had to take permission. Men were required to take permission of their parents. Unmarried girls were also required to take permission of their parents, but for married women, permission of their husbands was necessary, although married men did not required permission of their wives.[119]

### *Rules of conduct*

Generally, the rules of conduct for monks and nuns were similar. From the point of view of security, some restrictions were place on nuns like they could not go alone to ask for alms but had to go in groups of three or more. Preferably, a young nun was to go along with an old nun. Similarly, they could not go too far for this purpose. Generally, any contact of nuns with monks was restricted. They were not to touch each other or talk in private, but under unavoidable circumstances, exceptions were allowed.[120]

Controlled by these rules and disciplinary regulations, the nuns led a wandering life like that of the monks. In rainy season, they stayed in one place. The nuns were prevented from going beyond Amga-Magadha in the East, Kaushambi to the south, Sthuna to the west and Kunala in the north (roughly comprising the modern province of Bihar and U.P.), for "*so far extended the land of pious*".[121] The statement italicised indicates the orthodox hold of Jainas only in the area indicated. Probably the geographical limits belong to a period when Gujarat had not come under Jainism. However, it is quite likely that even after the religion had spread far and wide, Jainas continued to think of the area of Anga-Magadha, as more sacred, the true land of Jainas, just as Hindus considered the area of Aryavarta, extending from Punjab to Bengal, as the true land of Aryans.

## *Church administration*

A nun was call *bhikkuni, nigganthi, sahuni or ajjaa.* Nuns as a whole were always treated as inferior in relation to monks. It is said that a monk of three years standing may become the *upadhyaya* of a nun of thirty years standing and a monk of five years standing can become the *upadhyaya* of a nun of sixty years.[122]

The order of the nuns was under the control of monks. *Acharya, upadhyaya* and *pravartini* were the protectors of nuns. *Acharya* was the protector and guide of a *bhikkuni sangha*. In case of difficulties, he was expected to manage and arrange for proper requisites and residence for nuns. The *acharya* was responsible for letting the *pravartini* know the nature of offences, which the nuns were to refrain from.[123]

*Upadhyaya (uvajjaya)*—was next to *acharya* and was taken to be one of the protectors of the nuns. He perhaps looked to the educational aspects of the groups.[124]

*Ganini*—according to *Brhatkalpabhasya*, a *ganini* was superior to *pravartini*. She was the head of a *gana* or a group of nuns, and looked after administrative and spiritual aspects.[125] For becoming a *ganini* high standard of moral qualities and a long study of scriptures was required.

*Pravartini*—the mention of this position is found in the *Chedasutras.* She used to be the head of a group of nuns and managed all their affairs.[126] A *pravartini* was supposed to know all the rules of conduct and about the punishment for transgression.

There were other offices of the nuns too like *ganavacchedini, abhiseka, theri, bhikkuni, kshullika* (a young nun who was not confirmed and was on probation)[127] Many of these terms are in common with the Buddhist Church.

There was yet another title, the *mahattaraa*. It was probably given to an aged and venerable *sadhvi* with a role that was both spiritual and administrative.[128] There was also a masculine counterpart of this title. The author of most of the *curni* commentaries was Jinadasagani *mahattara* (7th c. C.E). According to S.B. Deo, *mahattara* was used in epigraphs to denote an officer in local administration also.[129]

Out of all these offices and titles of *sadhvis,* those noted in epigraphic records are *ganini, sadhvi, pravartini and mahattaraa.*

**Study:** was an important item in the life of a nun. As soon as she was initiated in the order, she was given instructions in the sacred books of canon. During the canonical period curriculum of studies was more or less the same for both monks and nuns, but by the early medieval period nuns were debarred from the study of some texts like *Drishtivada* and some other texts, on the ground of their being fickle minded.[130] After the 12th or 13th century, they were not only debarred from the study of some of the Agamas but were also debarred from the right to deliver sermons.[131] However, as mentioned earlier in Chapter III, they got back some of their rights after the reform movement of Lokashah in the 15th century. Nevertheless, how many nuns, particularly of Murtipujaka sub-sect, could benefit from this reform is doubtful. Later on, under the impact of the reform and revivalist movements of the modern period, things started changing for the better.

In spite of this lacklustre attitude of Jainas towards the education of the nuns, a few of them rose above their lot and created a place for themselves in the pages of history. The names of a few nuns could be cited here. Gunasadhvi was born in Gujarat. She was a Sanskrit scholar and she translated voluminous works of Siddharshisuri, and *Upamiti Bhava Prapancha Katha*, into Sanskrit in a scholarly manner. Siddharsisuri had composed this work in 906 C.E.[132] Ananda *mahattaraa* and Virmati *ganini—Visheshavashyaka-Bhasya* was composed by *acharya* Jinabhadragani in the seventh century C.E. A commentary on this work consisting of thirty-seven thousand *shlokas* was composed by Maldhari Hemachandra in 1118 C.E. In this work, seven people helped the author. Out of these seven people, two were the above mentioned nuns. The author himself has acknowledged their help.[133] *Sadhvi* Gunashri composed *Guruguna Chauvisi* based on the life of *mahopadhyaya* Dharmamurty *suri* of Anchalgaccha, in Kapadvanja.[134] Kalyanamati *ganini*, who was initiated by her brother Jineshwara *suri* in 1248 C.E., was given the charge of a *pravartini*. By her religiosity and sweet nature, she encouraged many women to join the order of nuns. She was a *sadhvi* of Khartargaccha.[135] Dharmalaxmi *mahattaraa* was the disciple of Ratnasimha *suri*. The dignity of *mahattaraa* was conferred on her in 1444–45 C.E., when she was in her teens. She was a successful preacher and one of her disciples was Vivekashri. From this account of Dharmalaxmi *mahattaraa*, it seems that during period II, at least a few *sadhvis* engaged themselves in preaching.[136]

In the corpus of inscription collected for this research, there are very few references to nuns. In numerical terms, out of more than four thousand inscriptions, nuns find mention only in eleven (Table 2). Shvetambars believed that a woman was capable of attaining *arhatship* and allowed women to pursue the career of a nun, but they never thought of men and women as equals. In the matter of ecclesiastical organisation also, women were treated as inferior to men. Knowing this, one cannot expect to find as many references to nuns as those to monks, in the epigraphic sources. However, one does not expect to see so little epigraphic space being accorded to the nuns either. Nuns must have acted as spiritual guides to lay women and motivated them to donate, and therefore it is not unreasonable to expect to see at least a few records in which nuns were mentioned as motivators or preachers. However, no such reference is to be found after the 14th century. Up to 14th century visibility of women renouncers in epigraphic space is fair in terms of frequency. In the available records there are seven inscriptions (including three on the images of nuns) in which nuns find mention. *Sadhvi* Malayasundari has been referred to as the spiritual guide of a woman donor while *mahattaraa* Charitrashri finds mention as a motivator.

**Table 2**
*Women Renouncers in Epigraphs*

| *Source* | *Religious Affiliation* | *Name of the nuns* | *Mentioned as* | *Year* |
|---|---|---|---|---|
| *Nir*, p. 67 | Vijayatungacarya gaccha | Accupta ganini | Donor | Shaka sam 930 |
| *Vijayavallabha Smaraka Grantha* | Not mentioned | mahattaraa (personal name not given) | Image for Worship | 1205 V.S. |
| *Vijayavallabha Smaraka Grantha* | Not mentioned | Demati ganini | Image for Worship | 1255 V.S. |
| *Vijayavallabha Smaraka Grantha* | Not mentioned | Arya Padmasiri | Image for Worship | 1298 V.S. |
| *PJLS-II* No 522 | Not clear | Sadhvi Malaya Sundari | Spiritual Guide | 1361 V.S. |
| *JPLS*, 303A | Upakeshagaccha | Sadhvi Bhavaladevi | Donor | 1421 V.S. |
| *Shat*, 76 | Not mentioned | mahattaraa Caritrashri | Motivator | 1430 V.S. |
| *APJLS*, No 188 | Khartaragaccha | (i) Bhavamati ganini<br>(ii) Dharmaprabhaganini<br>(iii) Ratnasundari sadhvi | Pilgrims | 1494 V.S. |
| *APJLS*, No 214 | Palhanpuriya gaccha | (i) Pravartini vidyasumati<br>(ii) Ratnasundari | Pilgrims | 1603 V.S. |
| *APJLS*, No 205 | Lost | Sadhvi Nathi | Pilgrim | 1608 V.S. |
| *Shat*, 499 | Not mentioned | sadhvi Rajsiri, sadhvi Candanabala, sadhvi Devasiri | Their foot impressions are being sponsored | 1856 V.S. |

In contrast with period I, both the subsequent periods reflect withdrawal of women renouncers from epigraphic space if one is guided by statistical data. There are only three inscriptions out of more than 3,000 inscriptions of period II, in which nuns find mention, that too only as pilgrims. In period III also there is only one inscription in which three nuns are mentioned. However, this is a unique record because it tells us that a monk sponsored the foot impressions of three *sadhvis.* This of course is an exceptional case.

The position of nuns in the *sangha* could be seen at two levels. Firstly, how many women actually took advantage of the option of renouncing and became nuns, and if their number has increased or decreased, what were the reasons for this change? Secondly, what happened to those women who actually became nuns? Whether they were treated on par with the monks or not. What restrictions were placed on their study, preaching etc.?

From the above data it is very difficult to say how many women actually became nuns, but it certainly indicates not only their secondary, but also low position in comparison to monks. At least for period I, there are two references to nuns as motivator and spiritual guide. However, near silence of the sources, especially after the fourteenth century, speaks volumes about the position of women in the *sangha.* It indicates, on the one hand, that perhaps fewer women became nuns, and on the other hand, their position further deteriorated. It could be that the order of nuns became an appendage to the order of monks, and nuns lived under the control and shadow of the monks. Fewer women opting out could possibly be a positive indication about the improved life of *shravikas.* It is quite possible that their position in the household improved to some extent and so lesser number of women were required to leave their homes for worldly reasons such as widowhood.

In this chapter a picture of an ideal woman as found in the Jaina literary sources, has been drawn. To see how far these textual provisions were practiced in actual life, this ideal picture has been compared with the data collected from the epigraphic sources. Though epigraphic sources do not throw light on each and every aspect of women's lives, overall it has been observed that, to a considerable extent the prescribed norms were observed.

The property rights given to women were in actual practice also granted to them on many occasions. That the daughters of sonless fathers could inherit their fathers' properties is indicated by the use of the term *putrika* in a few records. In certain records, even when the term *putrika* is not used, the phraseology indicates that the donor was in fact sonless and therefore his daughter and her son were his inheritors. For example Jesa, the donor, has associated his daughter's son with him when normally men associated their sons and sons' sons with them.

In many cases, widows got their property rights. This can be inferred from the inscriptions of Tejalde and Harkunvar *sethani*.

Polygamy was an accepted norm and many times women maintained cordial relations with their co-wives, as was expected from them. The idealised picture of a wife who was virtuous, faithful and obedient to her husband was valued. Women were indoctrinated into this ideology.

A few references to nuns found in our sources indicate that the permission to opt out of the family life indeed was also given to them in actual practice.

However, the scriptural prescriptions were also at times disregarded. Jaina scriptures do not prescribe the practice of *sati*, but the *sati* inscription, which has been cited in chapter III, indicates cross-cultural influence. The women or the family concerned must have been under the strong influence of Brahmanical values. There is a possibility that a few more cases of the type have gone unrecorded.

Throughout the period of this study, the entire value system was surcharged with patriarchal ideals. Nevertheless, these ideals were not timeless and unchanging. Patriarchy was constantly being constituted and reconstituted. These ideological changes influenced the thinking of lay people and the renounces alike.

The changes that have been observed in the pattern of identification (Table 3) as well as other changes cannot be without the modification in the character of patriarchy. It has been noted that the changes in the identification pattern of men and women took place simultaneously.

**Table 3**

*Attributes of Identity: Jaina Women's Preferences*

| *Attributes of Identity* | *Period I* | | *Period II* | | *Period III* | |
|---|---|---|---|---|---|---|
| | *No.* | *%* | *No.* | *%* | *No.* | *%* |
| Wifely | 32 | 43% | 306 | 71% | 24 | 43% |
| Daughterly | 19 | 25% | 59 | 14% | 7 | 13% |
| Both | 4 | 5% | 30 | 7% | 2 | 4% |
| Only Personal | 15 | 20% | 21 | 5% | 20 | 36% |
| Any Other | 5 | 7% | 12 | 3% | 3 | 4% |
| Total | 75 | 100% | 428 | 100% | 56 | 100% |

For period I it has been observed that women used their wifely as well as daughterly attribute of identity. When they used the daughterly attribute in most cases it was with reference to father alone. Similarly, in most cases, men identified themselves with reference to father or the male lineage, though some of them did give the names of their mothers and other female ancestors.

It could be inferred that women retained their identity as daughters and maintained relations with their parents. But parentage was traced, in most cases, with reference to father alone.

In period II women mostly identified themselves using their wifely attribute while men, almost always as a rule, identified themselves with reference to both the parents. Another observation of this period is a large number of group donations in which members of the patriarchal joint family donated together. Thus, it seems that the patriarchal joint families became stronger. The role of women as wives became very important. However, they did not altogether break relations with their parents. This is clear from some inscriptions in which we find women associating themselves with their brothers, sisters and other members of their natal family.

In period III the importance was still being given to women as wives, but a considerable proportion of women as well as men preferred not to use any familial attribute at all, indicating that a sense of self-identity as independent persons was growing.

The percentage of women donors was not constant. It fluctuated throughout the period of the study. From Table 1 (Chapter 1) it can be seen that the number of women donors (also men donors) was the highest in the 15th century, indicating that the trend of donating images was the highest in this century. However, the percentage of women donors was the highest in the 18th century; in other words, proportion of women donors to men donors was the highest in the 18th century—a century of socio-political turmoil. The epigraphic space which the women got was the least in 13th and 14th centuries and was the most in 17th, 18th and 19th centuries.

Another thing worth noting about the women donors is that for period I there is no epigraphic record of a big donation by any women. However, from period II onwards, i.e., 15th century onwards, there are a few epigraphic records, which tell us that women financed the construction or the renovation of the temples, or contributed large sums for the consecration ceremonies and other festivals.

Change in the attitude of the people towards nuns is also noticeable. While the epigraphic space, which the laywomen got, saw a gradual rise, the epigraphic space allotted to nuns was shrunk. Similarly, the capacity in which the nuns find mention also changed.

It can be seen that the changes taking place after period I are sharper than those taking place after period II and these seem to be related to the property rights of women.

- Reduced use of the daughterly attribute by the women after 14th century and simultaneous increase in the use of wifely attribute, indicating perhaps the reduced dependence of women on their fathers
- Improved status of women as wives in period II, which is indicated by their inclusion in the group donations as the associate donors

- Men in period II almost always identifying themselves with reference to their fathers as well as mothers, indicating improved status of mothers
- Gradual rise in the percentage of women donors
- Appearance of women donors donating large sums from period II onwards
- Nuns occupying less epigraphic space after period I, indicating that either the status of the nuns vis-à-vis monks had gone down or the number of nuns had reduced or both. It is quite likely that number of widows opting to become nuns had gone down because of the improved status of wives.

All the above points suggest that perhaps women as wives had been empowered to a certain extent after period I. As noted before, Hemachandra wrote *Arhanniti*, the only Shvetambara text on Jaina law, in 12th century. This law made wife the first heir of her husband's property. It is quite possible that this law, or at least this particular provision of the Jaina law, was put into practice some time later, probably in the 15th century. This is the time when Lokashah initiated his reforms. As a result of these reforms, the Sthanakavasi sect came into existence. However, Murtipujakas might have also been influenced by these reforms to some extent and on a few aspects. Though most of these reforms were religious in nature, it is likely that at this time, Shvetambara Jaina women got back their property rights, which is why, probably most of the records of women giving big donations come from this period. Similarly, withdrawal of nuns from the epigraphic space might also be related to this.

Thus, it seems that the Jaina law or its provision making wives the first heirs was fully put into practice some time in 15th century. This law, it seems, was at least partly responsible for bringing about the above mentioned changes.

In short, it can be said that in period I, role of women as wives was important but not highly stressed and the nuns, though to a limited extent still played a role as motivators and spiritual guides to lay women. From period II onwards the role of women as wives came to be greatly stressed, women as wives seem to have been empowered to a certain extent, and nuns were relegated to the background, under the shadow of monks. In period III too, role of women as wives remained their most important role but some sense of individuality among the women (as well as men) is visible.

In the end it could be said that the epigraphic sources not only bring out the distance or proximity between the prescribed norms and actual practice, but they also provide us with some additional information, which otherwise we do not get from the literary sources.

During the period of this study, to a great extent, Jaina women of Gujarat followed prescribed norms, which were essentially patriarchal in nature. However, modification in the character of patriarchy did take place from time to time. These modifications are reflected in the epigraphic records.

## Notes

1. *Encyclopaedia Americana*, Vol. 9, 2001 p. 50.
2. *Encyclopaedia of Religion and Ethics*, Vol. 4, 1935 p. 702.
3. *The New Encyclopaedia Britannica Inc.*, 1997 p. 56.
4. R. Williams, *Jaina Yoga* (Delhi: Motilal Banarasidas, 1983), p. xx.
5. Vilas Adinath Sangave, *Jaina Religion and Community* (California: Long Beach Publications, 1997), p. 43.
6. Hiralal Jain, "Jainism: Its History, Principals and Precepts" in *Studies in Jainism* (Calcutta: The Ramakrishna Mission Institute of Culture, 1997), pp. 26–27.
7. Hiralal Jain, "Literature of Jainism", in *Studies in Jainism* (Calcutta: The Ramakrishna Mission Institute of Culture, 1997), p. 70.
8. S.B. Deo, "History of Jain Monachism" in the *Bulletin of the Deccan College, Research Institute,* June 1954-March, 1955 p. 18.
9. Ibid., pp. 17–21.
10. Hiralal Jain, op. cit., p. 74.

11. Mohanlal Mehta, *Jaina Culture* (Varanasi: P.V. Research Institute, 1969), pp. 24–26.
12. Nalini Joshi, *Jaina Agamat Stri* (Pune: Dr K.K. Jain, 2000), pp. 34–35.
13. Mohanlal Mehta, op. cit., pp. 30–31.
14. Sagarmal Jain, "Jaina Dharma men Nari Ki Bhoomika" in *Jaina Dharma Ki Pramukha Sadviyam evem Mahilayem* by Hirabai Boradiya (Varanasi: P.V. Research Institute, 1991), p. 2.
15. Mohanlal Mehta, op. cit., p. 38.
16. S.B. Deo, op. cit., p. 37.
17. Mohanlal Mehta, op. cit., p. 33.
18. Ibid., pp. 34–36.
19. Ibid., pp. 39–41.
20. C.R. Jain, *The Jaina Law* (Madras: The Devendra Printing and Publishing Co. Ltd., 1926), p. 3 and 4.
21. Ibid., p. 4.
22. Ibid., pp. 6–10.
23. Muni Jinavijaya (ed.), Hariprasadaji Dwivedi, tran, *Shri Merutungachary Viracita Prabandhachintamani* (Ahmedabad, Calcutta: Sighi Jaina Grantha Mala, 1940), pp. 1–6.
24. Mohanlal Mehta, op. cit., p. 42.
25. *Jaina Stri Sadbodhaa* (Mehasana: Shri Jaina Shreyaskar Mandal,1933).
26. R.L. Raval, *Socio-Religious Movements in Gujarat (during 19th c)* (Delhi: Ess Ess Publications, 1987), p. 155.
27. Vilas Adinath Sangave, *Jaina Community: A Social Survey*, (Bombay: Popular, 1959).
28. Sagarmal Jain, op. cit.
29. Hirabhai Boradiya, *Jaina Dharma Ki Pramukha Sadhviyam evam* Mahilayem (Varanasi: P.V. Research Institute, 1991).
30. Nalini Joshi, op. cit.
31. S.B. Deo, op. cit., p. 493.
32. Vilas Adinath Sangave, op. cit., p. 177.
33. Sagarmal Jain, op. cit., p. 10.
34. Nalini Joshi, op. cit., p. 46.

35. Ibid.
36. Sagarmal Jain, op. cit., pp. 20–21.
37. Vilas Adinath Sangave, op. cit., p. 192.
38. Nalini Joshi, op. cit., pp. 48–49.
39. Satyapal Narang, *Hemachandras's Dvyashrayakavya*: A *Literary and Cultural Study* (New Delhi: Munshiram Manoharlal, 1972), pp. 185–88.
40. Kamta Prasad Jain, "Marriage in Jaina Literature", *Studies in Jainism* (Calcutta: The Ramakrishna Mission Institute of Culture, 1997), pp. 143.
41. *Jaina Stri Sadbodha* (Mehasana: Shri Jaina Shreyaskar Mandal, 1933), pp. 59–60.
42. Sagarmal Jain, op. cit., p. 35.
43. *Jaina Stri Sadbodha* (Mehasana: Shri Jaina Shreyaskar Mandal, 1933), p. 1.
44. Ibid.
45. Ibid.
46. C.R. Jain, op. cit., pp. 189–90.
47. Ibid., p. 178.
48. P.V. Kane, *History of Dharmashastra*—Vol. II, pt I (Poona: Bhandarkar Oriental Research Institute, 1941), p. 345.
49. C.R. Jain, op., cit., p. 200.
50. Ch II, Citation no. 7, 'Women with daughterly attribute of identity'.
51. Ch III, Citation no. 9, 'Men's inscriptions'.
52. Sagarmal Jain, op. cit., p. 24.
53. Nalini Joshi, op. cit., pp. 82–83.
54. Vilas Adinath Sangave, *Jain a Community: A Social* Survey, 2nd edition (Bombay: Popular, 1980), p. 81.
55. Ibid., pp. 65, 73
56. Muni Jinavijayaji, (ed.), *PJLS-II* Inscription no. 110–11, pp. 50–68, 107–8.
57. Nalini Joshi, op. cit., p. 82.
58. Ibid., p. 52.
59. Ibid., p. 61.

60. *TSPC* Vol. III, p. 167.
61. Nalini Joshi, op. cit., p. 61.
62. Ibid., p. 56.
63. Chapter III, Citation no. 13 and 22, 'Women with wifely attribute of identity'.
64. Chapter IV, 'Hemabhai's inscription at Shatrunjaya'.
65. *Jaina Stri Sadbodhaa,* p. 70.
66. *TSPC* Vol. IV, 1954, p. 54.
67. *Jaina Stri Sadbodha*, p. 31.
68. Chapter.II, Citation no. 9, 'Women with wifely attribute of identity'.
69. C.R. Jain, op. cit., pp. 205–6.
70. Ibid., p. 179.
71. Ibid., pp. 49, 178.
72. Ibid., p. 178.
73. See Chapter IV, Citation no. 1, 'Women with wifely attribute of identity'.
74. Nalini Joshi, op. cit., p. 59.
75. *Jaina Stri Sadbodha*, p. 67.
76. C.R. Jain, op. cit., p. 178.
77. C.R. Jain, op. cit., pp. 189–90.
78. Ibid., p. 184.
79. Nalini Joshi, op. cit., p. 63.
80. Ibid., p. 62.
81. Muni Jinavijayaji (ed.), Hariprasaji Dwivedi trans, *Prabandhachintamani*, Hin. 1940, p. 2.
82. Merutungacharya, C.H Tawney, tran, *The Prabandhachintamani or Wishing Stone of Narratives.* (Eng) (Calcutta: Asiatic Society, 1901), p. 154.
83. *Jaina Stri Sadbodha*, p. 123.
84. Nalini Joshi, op. cit., p. 69, 70.
85. Hemachandracharya, Helen M. Johnson, trans.*TSPC* Vol. III, 1949, p. 143.
86. Ibid.

87. Chapter III, 'Sati inscription'.
88. C.R. Jain, pp. 189–90.
89. Ibid., p. 184.
90. Ibid.
91. Ibid.
92. Ibid., p. 190.
93. Ibid., p. 191.
94. Ibid., p. 178.
95. Ibid., p. 198.
96. Ibid., p. 184.
97. Muni Jinavijayaji (ed.), Hariprasaji Dwivedi, trans, *Prabandhachintamani*, (Hin) 1940, pp. 104, 156.
98. C.B. Sheth, *Jainism in Gujarat* (Bombay: Shri Vijayadevsur Sangh Gyan Samiti, 1953), pp. 270–71.
99. Chapter IV, Citation no. 6, 'Women with wifely attributes of identity'.
100. Chapter III, Citation no. 23, "Woman with wifely attributes of identity" and its analysis.
101. Sagarmal Jain, "Brahmanic and Shramanik Cultures: A Comparative Study", *Studies in Jainism* (Calcutta: The Ramkrishan Mission Institute of Culture,1997), p. 86.
102. Nalini Joshi, op. cit., p. 19.
103. Padmanabh S. Jaini, *Gender and Salvation* 1st Indian edition (New Delhi: Munshiram Manoharlal Publishers Pvt. Ltd.,1992), p. 1.
104. Appasvami Chakravarti, "Jainism: Its Philosophy and Ethics", *Studies in Jainism* (Calcutta: The Ramkrishna Mission Institute of Culture, 1997), p. 54.
105. Ibid., p. 55.
106. Nalini Joshi, op. cit., pp. 117–19.
107. Appasvami Chakravarti, op. cit., p. 56.
108. Nalini Joshi, op. cit., p. 119.
109. Ibid., pp. 120–21.
110. Hirabhai Boradiya, *Jaina Dharma ki Pramukha Sadhviyam evam Mahilayem* (Varanasi: P.V. Research Institute, 1991), pp. 187–88.
111. Ibid., p. 189.

112. Ibid., p. 193.
113. Ibid., p. 194.
114. Sagarmal Jain, op. cit., p. 13.
115. Nalini Joshi, op. cit., pp. 120–21.
116. R.Williams, *Jaina Yoga* (Delhi: Motilal Banarasidass Publishers Pvt. Ltd., 1983) p. 165.
117. S.B. Deo, op. cit., pp. 465–66.
118. Nalini Balbir, "Women and Jainism in India" in *Women in Indian Religions* (ed.) by Arvind Sharma, (New Delhi: OUP, 2002), p. 89.
119. S.B. Deo, op. cit., p. 466.
120. Nalini Joshi, op. cit., pp. 112–13; Sagarmal Jaina, op. cit., pp. 39–40.
121. S.B. Deo, op. cit., pp. 473–74.
122. Ibid., p. 467.
123. Ibid., p. 468.
124. Ibid.
125. Ibid.
126. Ibid.
127. Ibid., pp. 470–71.
128. N. Shanta, *The Unknown Pilgrims*, 1st English edition (Delhi: Sri Satguru Publications, Delhi,1997), p. 178.
129. S.B. Deo, op. cit.
130. S.B. Deo, op. cit.
131. Sagarmal Jain, op. cit., p. 37.
132. Hirabhai Boradiya, op. cit., p. 186.
133. Ibid., p. 193.
134. Ibid., p. 196.
135. Ibid.
136. C.B. Sheth, op. cit., pp. 221–22.

# 6

# Conclusion

## I

The main purpose of this research was to study Jaina women taking into account, as far as possible, their own experiences. It was intended to see whether the liberal attitude adopted by the Jainas, as compared to the attitude of Hindus, was practiced or not. It was also intended to see how much space was available to Jaina women within the patriarchal framework, that is to say, whether the patriarchal norms were flexible enough to allow women some freedom and agency. Lastly, an attempt was made to throw some light on the gender relations in the Jaina community of Gujarat.

For this, the epigraphic sources were used. On arranging the epigraphic data chronologically, a broad pattern was visible. Based on this pattern a scheme of periodisation was prepared, dividing the available epigraphic data into three distinct periods in terms of centuries covered by them. During the course of the study, it was noted that broadly, these periods also indicated some change in the patriarchal values. (17th century inscriptions however, show the features of both period II as well as period III.)

## II

At the end of this exercise, the following conclusions were arrived at:

1. As far as the epigraphic evidence indicates, the liberal attitude adopted by the Jainas of Gujarat towards their women was, to a considerable extent, also practiced in actual life.

Jainism gave women the option of renouncing the world and becoming nuns. Throughout the period of the study, it can be noted that women indeed took advantage of this option and became nuns. The references to nuns in the inscriptions, though very few, indicate the presence of the order of nuns.

On many occasions, women got the property rights due to them. According to the Jaina law a widow, whether she had a son or not, could inherit her deceased husband's property. In actual practice also probably, on many occasions, especially after period I, widows were granted the property rights due to them. Similarly, it seems that the only daughters of sonless fathers could inherit his property.

The four-fold Jaina *sangha* consists of *sadhus, sadhvis, shravakas* and *shravikas*. Thus, women had a place of their own, though secondary, in this structure as *sadhvis* and *shravikas*, which they retained throughout the period of this study. Jaina laymen and laywomen, that is *shravakas* and *shravikas*, considered donating for the cause of the religion as a pious deed. *Shravikas* were quite enthusiastic about their religious duties and made donations, but the percentage of women donors or the proportion of women donors in relation to men donors was not the same always. The epigraphic space, which the women occupied, has always been fluctuating. However, this percentage shows a rising trend from period II onwards. The percentage of women donors is the least in the 13th and 14th centuries, which was considered to be the golden period in the history of Gujarat, and the most in 18th century, a period of socio-political turmoil (refer to the Table 1 in Chapter 1). This indicates that periods of peace and stability strengthen the hold of patriarchy. Furthermore it seems that *shravikas* as a group became more active from period II onwards. This is indicated by two inscriptions belonging to period II and period III respectively, where donations were made by groups of *shravikas.* It therefore seems that they occasionally came together for religious purposes and made donations. Once their groups were formed, it is likely that they might also have come together for social purposes. It is true that there are only two such inscriptions and '*shravika* groups' may not have been a common thing, nevertheless there certainly must have been some such groups.

However, on certain occasions, religious prescription being disregarded can be noted. Jainism does not support the practie of *sati* and by and large, and Jainas did not practice *sati,* but a single epigraph making mention of three Jaina *satis*, as mentioned in chapter III, indicates that at times *sati* might have been practised by a few Jainas influenced by the Brahmanical values.

On many other counts, the position of Jaina women was no different from their Hindu sisters. Child marriage, polygamy, bar on widow remarriage, lack of education, and other such things made their lives quite difficult.

2. As noted above, the Jainas of Gujarat generally followed the religious prescriptions and did give women the space allotted to them. It has also been noted that on certain occasions the prescribed norms were disregarded, as for example in the case of *sati.* But in this case the deviation from the norm resulted in further shrinking of the women's space. In case of nuns also we find that the space given to them was shrunk considerably after 14th century when nuns as motivators or spiritual guides, disappear from the epigraphic space. Similarly, they were also barred from the study of certain texts. In contrast to this, the percentage of women donors slowly went up from period II onwards. Moreover, a few women donating large sums for the construction of new temples or other such purposes appear on the scene. The property rights of women seem to have been enlarged from period II onwards.

Thus, the space allowed to women was shrunk in certain areas while in others there was some enlargement of the space available to them.

3. Some observations about the gender relations in the Jaina community of Gujarat can also be made based on the inscriptional sources. Daughters occupied less space in the familial worlds of their fathers, probably because they were married early in life. From the daughters' point of view it could be said that in period fathers were still quite important figures after their husbands for the daughters. After period I, however, the importance of fathers vis-à-vis husbands seems to have been reduced. Perhaps they were now less dependent on their fathers.

Brothers and sisters also occupied less space in each other's lives. However, the relationship between brothers and sisters seems to be of equitable nature.

In contrast to the brother-sister relationship, relations between husband and wife were not of equitable nature, wives were not only considered subordinate to their husbands, but the presence of polygamy indicates that they were looked upon as possessions rather than as partners. Nevertheless, on some occasions, when the wife was the only daughter of her father and therefore an heir to his property, these norms of husband-wife relations were not followed or at times even reversed.

The literature attributes high status to mothers. Epigraphic records indicate that in practice also mothers commanded high respect from their sons. In the familial hierarchy, they were accorded higher positions than their sons. The respect shown by the sons towards their mothers was not just a gesture without mothers holding any real power. The legal provisions making women the first heirs to their husbands' property helped them in retaining their advantaged position. For this reasons, even when the women were not widowed, they seem to have held a latent power over their sons. Such must have been the case where the woman was either the first or the only wife of her husband, as it was the eldest wife who was the heir to her husband's property.

Thus, though slight variations in gender relations are noticeable over the centuries, on the whole it could be said that gender relations were governed by the norms of familial hierarchy.

4. So far it has been noted that in most of the cases there was very little difference between the prescriptions and practice. The entire value system was loaded with patriarchal ideals. However, these ideals were not unchanging and modifications in these ideals are noticeable. Patriarchy was being reconstituted time and again. As a result of this, as noted above, importance of father was reduced vis-à-vis husband to a certain extent after period I. These modifications also altered the way both women themselves and society at large, looked at them.

During period I the role of women as wives was important but not so highly stressed. The nuns, although to a limited extent, still played a role as motivators and spiritual guides to lay women.

During period II the role of women as wives came to be greatly stressed and the nuns were relegated to the background. Patriarchal families perhaps became stronger and status of women, as wives seems to have improved to some extent.

During period III the role of women as wives was still their most important role, but some sense of individuality is noticeable among the Jaina women (as well as men) of this period. The order of nuns continued to exist but remained in the background.

"Women's history", according to Gerda Lerner, "must contain not only the activities and events in which women participated, but the record of changes in their perception of themselves and their roles".[1] To some extent, this work has tried to fulfil this expectation.

## III

The scope of this study is limited to 11th-19th centuries of our era. In the last century of this period, that is the 19th century, British rule was established in India.

With the establishment of the British rule, the Indian society was confronted with an entirely a different kind of heterogenetic cultural tradition.[2] The criticism of the Indian culture by the

Europeans, especially the missionaries and the colonial writers like James Mill, had a twin effect on Indians. One was the starting of the socio religious reform movements in the 19th century and the other was the emergence of the nationalist historiography.

The nationalist historians were constructing a particular kind of past. In this new script, women's history found an important place.[3] This was because the position of women came be considered as the index of civilisations. The high status of women in the Vedic age was emphasised. Women were seen essentially within the context of the family and the picture of women as ideal wife and ideal mother was created.

The issues which attracted the 19th century reformers were *sati,* widow remarriage, education of women and other such issues related to women, apart from the issue of caste discrimination. The reformers advocated humanitarian changes in the positions of women. They advocated the changes in the position of women in order to make them good wives and mothers.

Thus patriarchy was being reconstituted again to suit the needs of the 19th century. Along with Hindus, Jainas also went through the same process. Among the wealthy people who supported reforms by their generous donations, there were many Jaina merchants also. The book *Jaina Stri Sadbodha,* referred to in the precious chapter, is one of the books which tried to infuse the new value into popular mind. The books also quoted from the *Agamas* and other scriptures to show that the position of women had been good in the ancient period and advocated changes in the position of women so that they could became good wives and mothers. The sixteen *satis* of the Jaina tradition like Sita, Draupadi and Damayanti were projected as role models for women.

The effect of these reformist activities became visible only in the 20th century and therefore they are not reflected in the inscriptional records of the 19th century. Women started getting education, the age of marriage was slowly going up and many women came out to participate in the struggle for freedom. These changes, which seemed like radical changes, were essentially only conservative in nature. Women were kept within the structural confines of family and society. The patriarchal social structure remained intact. The concept of gender equality probably did not exist at that time.

In spite of these limitations of the reform movements, there is no denying the fact that they proved beneficial to women. The pace of progress increased after independence. The Hindu Marriage Act of 1955 and Hindu Succession Act of 1956 were instituted. Polygamy became illegal, the age of marriage was raised to eighteen for girls and twenty-one for boys, and women could file for separation and divorce.[4] All the above laws were also applicable to the Jainas. These constitutional changes definitely benefited women. Patriarchal norms began to be observed with less severity. But still by and large, the subordinate position of women has persisted. The feminist movement of the seventies of this era has been able to bring about a change in the mindset of some people. Because of this, a section of the population has started thinking in terms of 'gender equality'. However, the Jaina society of Gujarat, much like the rest of the Indian communities, has remained patriarchal in nature. The long history of subordination of women is highlighted by the two epigraphs, which could be referred to here.

The first epigraph is dated 1298 V.S. (1242 C.E.). It is a record of the resolutions of a council of Shvetambara Jaina monks and laymen. The resolutions were passed in order to check the slackness in the behaviour of the renouncers staying in the *caityas* and *vasatis* of Gujarat.[5]

The second epigraph, dated V.S. 2032 (1976 C.E.), tells us about the building of a new temple, the installation of images in it and the consecration ceremony that followed. These activities were undertaken by Kalyanaji Anandji *Sangha*. The Jainas who had come from all over India attended the ceremony. [6]

Though the purpose of both these records is different, they are similar on one count. They represent the collective activities of the Jaina community. This is the reason why they have been chosen to highlight the point here.

In both these records, women are conspicuous by their absence. The first record gives the name of many monks and laymen who were present and states that the resolution was passed in the presence of the four-fold *sangha*. Women are subsumed under the term, *chaturvidhashrisangha*.

In the second record names of many famous monks of the time, who were present, are mentioned. But the nuns find only a collective mention under the term *sadhunam cha sadhvinam cha sahastram samupasthitam* In 1976 C.E. there were a few very famous Jaina nuns and some of them must have attended this ceremony. Yet not even a single name of a nun is given.

Looking critically at all such events it can be seen that patriarchy has survived all through and succeeded in subordinating women. This long history of subordination can end only when the patriarchal social structure is replaced by some other system where no discrimination is made based on gender. Today, historical development has, for the first time, created the necessary conditions by which large groups of women—finally, all women—can emancipate themselves from subordination.[7] At present there are more Jaina women than ever before who are highly educated and are holding important positions in various educational and other institutions. Among the renouncers also, we find many highly educated nuns. Beyond the role of a wife or a mother, many life options are open to them. Woman today can be a wife or a mother and still pursue a career outside. Yet, going by the reading of the recorded past one simply hopes that patriarchy does not reconstitute itself to devise subtle means of imposing subordination blocking the march to liberation of women.

## Notes

1. Gerda Lerner, *The Majority Finds it's Past* (New York: OUP, 1979), pp. 160–61.
2. R.L. Raval, *Socio-Religious Movements in Gujarat (during 19th c)*. (New Delhi: Ess Ess Publications, 1987), p. 233.

3. Uma Chakravarti, "Whatever Happened to the Vedic Dasi" in Kumkum Sagari and Sudesh Vaid (ed.), *Recasting Women: Essays in Colonial History* (Delhi: Kali for Women, 1989; rpt, 1999), p. 27.
4. Katherine K. Young, "Women and Hinduism" in Arvind Sharma (ed.), *Women in Indian Religions* (New Delhi, OUP, 2002) p. 22.
5. U.P. Shah, "A Forgotten Chapter in the History of Shvetambara Jaina Church", in *Journal of the Asiatic Society of Bombay,* Vol. 30, pt I, 1955. pp. 100–113. This epigraph was incised on a slab at Mt. Shatrunjaya. It is not traceable now. The transcript made in the 15th century makes the text of the epigraph known to us. The manuscript copy of this was in the collection of Pravartaka Shri Kantivijayji).
6. *Shat*, part 4, p. 112, Inscription no — Purti-1.
7. Gerda Lerner, *The Creation of Patriarchy* (New York: OUP, 1979), p. 220.

# Bibliography

## Primary sources

### *Epigraphic*

Acharya, G.V., *Historical Inscriptions of Gujarat*, Vols. I, II and III, Mumbai: Forbes Gujarati Sabha, 1933, 1935 and 1942.

Acharya, Kanchansagarsuriji, (auth.) Muni Pramodsagar (ed.) *Shri Shatrunjaya Giriraja Darshana ane Shilpa Sthapatya Kalamam Shatrunjaya,* Kapadwanj: Agamoddharaka Grantha Mala, 1982.

Buddhisagarsuriji, *Jaina Dhatu Ptratima Lekha Sangraha,* Vols. I and II, Mumbai: Padra: Shri Adhyatmajnan Prasaraka Mandal, 1917, 1924.

Burges, J. et al. (eds.), *Epigraphia Indica,* Vols. I to XLII (Reprint)

Diskalkar, D.B., *Inscriptions of Kathiawar*, Bombay: Karnatak Publishing House, 1944.

Lodha, Daulatsingh, 'Arvinda' (ed.), *Shri Jaina Pratima Lekha Sangraha*, Dhanmaniya: Shri Yatindra Sahitya Sadana, 1951.

Muni, Jayantavijayaji (ed.), *Shri Arbuda Prachina Jaina Lekha Sangraha*, Ujjain: Shri Vijayadharmasuri Jaina Grantha Mala, 1937.

Muni, Jinavijayaji (ed.), *Prachina Jaina Lekha Sangraha,* Vol. II, Bhavnagar: Jaina Atmananda Sabha, 1921.

Muni, Vidyavijayaji (ed.), *Prachina Lekha Sangraha, I*, Bhavnagar: Shri Yashovijaya Grantha Mala, 1929.

Muni, Vishalvijayaji (ed.), *Shri Radhanapura Pratima Lekha Sandoha*, Bhavnagar: Shri Yashovijaya Grantha Mala, 1960.

Nahar, Purnachandra, *Jaina Lekha Sangraha* Part-I, Banaras: Jaina Vividha Sahityashastra Mala, 1918.

Shastri, H.G, *Historical Inscriptions of Gujarat*, Vols. IV and V, Mumbai: Forbes Gujarati Sabha, 1979, 1881.

### *Articles*

Shah, Ashita, "Bharuca se Prapta Jaina-Dhatu-Pratimaom ke Lekha", *Nirgrantha*, III, 1997–2002, pp. 344–48.

Shah, U.P., "Some Notable Shvetambara Jaina Bronzes", *Nirgrantha, III*, 1997–2002, pp. 66–69.

—, "A Forgotten Chapter in the History of Shvetambara Jaina Church", in the *Journal of the Asiatic Society of Bombay*, Vol. 30, pt I, 1955, pp. 100–113

### *Textual*

*Prabandhachintamani* composed by Merutungacharya, trans., (Hindi), Dwivedi, Pa. Hajariprasdaji, Ahmedabad: Singhi Jaina Grantha Mala, 1940.

*Prabandhachintamani*, composed by Merutungacharya, trans., (English) Tawney, C.R., Calcutta: Asiatic Society, 1901.

*Trishashtishalakapurushacharita*, composed by Hemachandracharya, trans, Johnson Helen M., Vols. I–IV, Baroda: Oriental Institute, G.O.S. 1931–1956.

## Secondary sources

### I

Parikh, Ramlal and Jamindar Rasesh, *Epigraphic Resources in Gujarat*, Delhi: Butala and Co., 1981.

Ramesh, K.V., *Indian Epigraphy*, Vol. I, Delhi: Sandeep Prakashan, 1984.

Salmon, Richard, *Indian Epigraphy*, Delhi: Munshiram Manoharlal, 1998.

Sircar, D.C., *Indian Epigraphy*, Delhi: Motilal Banarasidas, 1965.

—, *Indian Epigraphical Glossary*, Delhi: Motilal Banarasidas, 1966.

## II

Commissariat, M.S., *A History of Gujarat: Including a Survey of Chief Architectural Monuments and Inscriptions,* Vol. I, London: Longmans Green and Co., 1938

—, Vol. II, Bombay: Orient Longmans, 1957.

Desai, Neera, *Social Change in Gujarat: A Study of 19th c. Gujarat Society,* Bombay: Vroa & Co. Publishers Pvt. Ltd., 1978

Janaki, V.A., *Gujarat as the Arabs knew it (A Study in Historical Geography),* Baroda: M.S University, 1969.

Majumdar, M.R., *Cultural History of Gujarat,* Bombay: Popular Prakashan, 1965.

Rajyagor, S.B., *History of Gujarat,* New Delhi: S. Chand and Company Ltd., 1982.

Raval R.L., *Socio Religious Movements in Gujarat (during 19th c),* New Delhi: Ess Ess Publication, 1987.

Sankalia, H.D., *Archaeology of Gujarat,* Bombay: Natwarlal & Co., 1941.

—, *Studies in the Historical and Cultural Geography and Ethnography of Gujarat: Places and People in the Inscriptions of Gujarat 300 B.C.–1300 A.D.,* Poona: Deccan College P.G. and Research Institute, 1949.

Sheth, C.B., *Jainism in Gujarat (A.D. 1100–1600),* Bombay: Shri Vijaydevasursangha Gyan Samiti, 1953.

Shastri, H.G., *Gujaratno Prachina Itihasa,* Ahmedabad: Gujarat University, 1973.

## III

Basham, A.L., *The Wonder that was India,* London: Sidgwick & Jackson, 1954.

—, (ed.), *A Cultural History of India,* Delhi: OUP, 1975.

Kosambai, D.D., *Ancient India: A History of its Culture and Civilization,* New York: Pantheon Books, 1965.

Majumdar, R.C and Pusalkar, (General Editors), *The History and Culture of the Indian People,* Vol. V, *(The Sturggle for Empire),* Bombay: Bharatiya Vidya Bhavan, 1957.

Mukherjee, S.N. (ed.) *Indian History and Thought: Essays in Honour of A.L.Basham,* Calcutta: Subarnarekha, 1982.

Sankalia, H.D., *Aspects of Indian History and Archaeology,* Delhi; B.R. Publishing Corporation 1977.

Sircar, D.C., *Studies in the Religious Life of Ancient and Medieval India,* Delhi: Motilal Banarasidas, 1971.

Thapar, Romila, *Ancient Indian Social History*, New Delhi: Orient Longman, 1978.

—, *Narratives and the Making of History*, Delhi: OUP, 2000.

## IV

Babb, L.A., *Ascetics and Kings in a Jaina Ritual Culture*, 1st Indian Edition, Delhi: Motilal Banarasidas, 1998.

Bhadrabahu Vijay, *Guidelines of Jainism*, Mehasana: Shri Visvakalyan Prakashan Trust, 1986.

Bhattacharya, N.N., *Jaina Philosophy (Historical Outline)*, New Delhi: Munshiram Manoharlal, 1976.

Carrithers, Michal and Humphry Caroline, *The Assembly of Listeners: Jainas in Society*, Cambridge: Cambridge University Press, 1991.

Cort, John E., (ed.), *Scripture and Community: Collected Essays on the Jains*, Atlanta-Gerogia: Scholars Press, 1993.

—, *Jains in the World, Religious Values and Ideology in India*, New Delhi: OUP, 2001.

Deo, S.B., *History of Jaina Monachism from Inscriptions and Literature*, Poona: Deccan college 1956.

Dwivedi, R.C., *Contribution of Jainism to Indian Culture*, Varanasi: Motilal Banarasidas, 1975.

Gopalan, S., *Outlines of Jainism*, New Delhi: Wiley Eastern Pvt. Ltd., 1973.

Jain, Champat Rai, *The Jaina Law*, Madras: The Devendra Printing and Publishing Co. Ltd., 1926.

Jain, J.C., *Life in Ancient India: As depicted in Jaina Canons*, Bombay: New Book Co., 1965.

—, *The Jain Way of Life*, Gurgaon: The Academic Press, 1991.

Jain J.P., *The Jaina Sources of the History of Ancient India*, Delhi: Munshiram Manoharlal, 1964.

Jain, K.P., *Sankshipta Jaina Itihasa*, Surat: Mulchand Kisanchand Kapadia.

Jain, P.S., (ed.), *Medieval Jainism: Culture and Environment*, Delhi: Ashish Publishing House, 1990.

Jaini, P.S., *Gender and Salvation*, New Delhi: Munshiram Manoharlal, 1992.

Kapadia, H.R., *Canonical Literature of the Jains*, Surat: 1941.

Kulkarni, V.M., *A Treasury of Jaina Tales*, Ahmedabad: Shardaben Chimanbhai Educational Research Centre, 1994.

Laidlaw, James, *Riches and Renunciation: Religion, Economy and Society among the Jain,* Oxford: Clarendon Press, 1965.

Mehta, M.L, *Jaina Culture,* Varanasi: P.V. Research Institute, 1969.

Ramchandran, T.N., *Jaina Monuments and Places of First-Class Importance,* Calcutta: Virasasana Sangha, 1944.

Rangarajan, Hariyriya, et al. (eds.), *Jainism: Art Architecture, Literature and Philosophy,* Delhi: Sharada Publishing House, 2001.

Sangave, Vilas Adinath, *Jaina Community: A Social Survey,* Bombay: Popular, 1959.

—, *Jaina Religion and Community,* California: Long Beach, 1997.

Shah C.J., *Jainism in North India,* London: Longman and Green Co., 1932.

Singh, N.K., *Ideal, Ideology and Practice,* Jaipur: Printwell, 1987.

Williams, R., *Jaina Yoga: A Survey of Mediaeval Shravakacharas,* (repr), Delhi: Motilal Banarasidas, 1998.

## V

Altekar, A.S., *The Position of Women in Hindu Civilization: From Prehistoric Times to the Present Day,* 3rd edition, Delhi: Motilal Banarasidas, 1978.

Balbir, Nalini, "Women and Jainism in India", in Arvind Sharma edited, *Women in Indian Religions,* Indian edition, New Delhi: OUP, 2002.

Bhatta, Ilaben, *Gujaratni Nari,* Gandinagar: Government of Gujarat, 1974.

Boradiya, Hirabai, *Jaina Dharma Ki Pramukha Sadhviyam evam Mahilayem,* Varanasi, P.V. Research Institute, 1991.

Bose, Mandakranta, (ed.), *Faces of Feminine: In Ancient Medieval and Modern India,* Delhi: O.U.P, 2000.

Chakravarti, Uma and Kumkum Poy, "In Search of Our Past: A Review of the Limitations and Possibilities of the Historiography of Women in Early India" in *Economic and Political Weekly,* 23: p. ws 2–10, 1988.

—, "Whatever Happened to Vedic Dasi? "in Sangari Kumkum and Sudesh Vaid (eds.), *Recasting Women: Essays in Colonial History* (Reprint), New Delhi: Kali for Women, 1999.

—, "Beyond the Altekarian Paradigm: Towards a New Understanding of Gender Relations in Early Indian History", in Kumkum Roy (ed.), *Women in Early Indian Societies,* New Delhi: Manohar, 1999.

Desai, Neera and Maithrey, Krishnaraj, *Women and Society in India,* Delhi: Ajanta Publications, 1987.

*Jaina Stri Sadbodha*, Mehasana: Shri Jaina Shreyaskar Mandala, 1933.

Jain, Sagarmal, Jaina Dharma men Nari ki Bhoomika, in *Jaina Dharma Ki Pramukh Sadhviyam evam Mahilayem,* Varanasi, 1991.

Jayawardena, Kumari, *Feminism and Nationalism in the Third World,* New Delhi: Kali for Women, 1986.

Joshi, Nalini, *Jaina Agamat Stri*, Pune: K.K. Jain, 2000.

Krishnaraj, Maithreyi, "Evolving New Methodologies in Research on Women's Studies", in *Contribution to Women's Studies Series–3*, Mumbai: R.C.W.S., S.N.D.T.

Lerner, Gerda, *Majority Finds its Past*, New York: OUP, 1979.

– -, *The Creation of Patriarchy*, Oxford: OUP, 1986.

Mies, Maria, *Indian Women and Patriarchy,* New Delhi: Concept Publishing Co, 1980.

Muni, Yashovijaya, "Jaina Sadhvijioni Bhavya Pashana Pratimao" in Sandesara Bhogilal et al. edited, *Acharyaa Shri Vijayavallabhasuri Smaraka Grantha,* Mumbai: Shri Mahavira Jaina Vidyalaya, 1956.

Nicholson, Linda, (ed.) *Feminism/Postmodernism,* New York: Routledge, 1990.

Perrot, Michelle, (ed.) *Writing Women's History*, trans., Pheasant Felicia Oxford: Blackwell, 1992.

Pyarchandhji Maharaja, *Jaina Jagat Ki Mahilayem*, Ratlam: Shri Jainodaya Pustaka Samiti, 1949.

Roy, Kumkum, (ed.), "*Women in Early Indian Societies,* New Delhi, Manohar, 1999.

Sangari Kumkum, Sudesh Vaid, *Women and Culture,* Mumbai: R.C.W.S., S.N.D.T, 1994.

Scott, J.W., *Feminism and History,* New York: OUP, 1996.

Shah, K.K., *The Problem of Identity: Women in Early Indian Inscriptions,* New Delhi: OUP, 2001.

Shanta, N., *The Unknown Pilgrims, The Voices of Sadhvis: The History, Spirituality and Life of Jaina Women Ascetics,* Trans, Rogers Mary, Delhi: Shri Sadguru Publications, 1997.

Sharma, Arvind, (ed.), *Women in Indian Religions,* Indian edition, New Delhi: OUP, 2002.

Swami, Madhavanand, Majumdar R.C., (ed.), *Great Women of India,* Himalayas: Advaita Ashram, 1953.

Thomas, P., *Indian Women Through the Ages,* Bombay: Asia Publishing House, 1964.

# Index